"What the world needs now
is Love Sweet Love..."

Other books by Larry Crane and Lester Levenson

The Way to Complete Freedom

The Ultimate Truth about Love and Happiness

No Attachments. No Aversions. Autobiography of Lester Levenson

The Final Step to Freedom

The Power of Love

The Abundance Book, the Amazing Release Technique

LOVE YOURSELF

And let the other person have it your way

Lawrence Crane

From the teachings of Lester Levenson

Library of Congress designation SRu880-047 as of July 23,2008.

Publisher:
Release Technique, LP
15101 Rayneta Drive
Sherman Oaks, CA 91403

Phone: 818-279-2438
Fax: 818-385-0563

Email: ReleaseLA@aol.com
Web site: www.releasetechnique.com

ISBN No. 978-0-9778726-1-9

Printed in the United States of America

Library of Congress designation SRu880-047 as of July 23, 2008.

The publisher and author of this material make no medical claims for its use. This material is not intended to treat, diagnose or cure any illness. If you need medical attention please consult with your medical practitioner.

Let the Other Person Have it Your Way

When you are loving, people come your way. They give you what you want. They may not know why they did it. But they feel something special about you. They want to let you have it your way. They're compelled by love. They feel the power of love. In this book, you too will learn how to let the other person have it your way. You will learn, when you give love, when you are loving, the entire world comes your way.

This book is dedicated to

Lester Levenson

Lester Levenson is the originator of the Release Technique. Lester was a man from Elizabeth, New Jersey. He was the same kind of person as you and all of the rest of us on the planet, until he discovered what you are about to find out about in this book.

Lester was a physicist and an engineer. He had the book learning. He was well read and had a vast amount of worldly knowledge. However, all of that failed to give him what he wanted. He wanted happiness and went about trying to find it just like everybody does. Whatever he tried in his pursuit of happiness, he ended up in the same place of unhappiness and searching.

As you are about to find out, all of that changed when Lester made a simple, yet marvelously transforming discovery. Lester found out what it takes to be completely happy. He spent the rest of his life sharing what he found out with others. In this book, I am sharing Lester's discovery with you.

Lester was a kind, giving and caring person. People sought him out just to be around him. They could sense that he knew something they should know. They wanted to somehow share in the goodness they felt emanating from Lester.

Thousands of people's lives have been changed, and they have been able to find the happiness that Lester found using what he discovered.

It is for you, and all of those that have been touched by his teachings, that we gratefully dedicate this book to Lester Levenson.

Contents

LOVE YOURSELF

There are no Impossibles

Lester Levenson showed us that there are no impossibles. Nothing is impossible.

What would you like to have? You can have that and more if you learn to love yourself. What would you like to do? You can do that and more if you learn to love yourself. What would you like to be? You can be that and more if you learn to love yourself.

Love yourself, and for you nothing is impossible.

When you learn about love you will find that you have the most powerful tool available to you all the time. Love is the answer. Love is healing. Love is transforming. Love resolves. Love is curative. Love can repair anything or anyone. Love is strength. Love is power.

Love is the solution. Love is the answer. When you learn to love yourself the world is yours. When you learn to love yourself you live in the highest energy. When you learn to love yourself you live in the highest feeling possible.

When you learn to love yourself you can have everything. You can have everything and anything even if it might seem unattainable to you right now. The world comes your way when you love yourself. People come your way. Money comes your way. Health comes your way. Success comes your way. Happiness comes your way. Everything in your life works perfectly when you love yourself.

I was a salesman. One day, on a sales call, I was told I was going to lose a million dollar order. I went back to my room and began to apply love to the situation and send love to the buyer who had dropped the order. I got to the place of love for all concerned. The next morning, the same buyer called me and told me he had re-considered. He gave me an order for $3 million dollars which gave me a million dollar profit. I then began to apply love in all areas of my life. I got rid of bad asthma I had for over 20 years. My relationships with women became fantastic. I started to double and triple my investments. I'm now retired and traveling the world. Applying love is amazing and effective. It changed my life.

— Jim Whitman, World Traveler

Schools Don't Teach You About Love.

You went to school for a long time. Some people went to school for a large percentage of their life. Yet, not one person ever had a course on love, even if they've got several Ph.D.'s. Schools don't teach how to love. They don't teach what love is. They don't teach what is most important. Which is, what it takes to be loving. They don't teach that you achieve happiness through love.

You will find what love is and how to get it in this book.

Love is almost universally misunderstood. People don't know what love really is. The world thinks it knows what love is. But when you take a close look, what the world thinks is love, is not love at all. It's just the opposite. It's what can you do for me? If I love you, I expect something in return. If you don't give me what I want, I don't love you.

Lester Levenson learned about love. He learned where to find love. He learned how to apply love in his life. I will show you what Lester showed me. I'll share Lester's own words about love with you. I'm talking about the real love, the love that brings you everything your heart desires.

The World Has it Backwards

Most of the people in the world are pursuing the opposite of love. Lester referred to it as non-love. They practice non-love, and they hurt themselves and others more and more everyday.

Most of the billions on the planet live their days and their lives in non-love. You don't have to go very far to see it. Turn on the television. Turn to one of the news channels. That's as far as you have to go to find out about non-love.

Most of the people on the planet tip the scale toward non-love. They don't like this or that. They don't like him or her. They oppose that group in favor of this group. They live their lives feeling threatened by other people. They live their lives feeling threatened by imagined forces. They don't understand who or what they are. They just know they don't like them. It's living in hate in varying degrees. Kindness does not rule this world. You don't have to look very far to see that.

Most everyone is playing defense. "I have to protect myself, so they don't hurt me, so they don't take away what I have, so they don't take away my life." They set up all of this opposition. "I oppose her because she does this or that." "I oppose that group of people because they have beliefs that are contrary to mine."

It's non-loving behavior. It's non-loving thinking. It's non-loving acting.

> *Seven years ago I was managing a pizzeria. I made $30,000 a year and all the pizza I could eat. (Fortunately it was good pizza.) I learned this technique and started applying it seriously. It happened so easily – now I own my own business, have a wonderful lifestyle, and have a multimillion-dollar net worth. And I'm so much happier than I've ever been.*
>
> **— Steven Winn, Iowa**

The answer to all of this is love.

The answer is to love everyone and everything.

Most people in the world have it completely backwards. Most people think hating somehow protects them. The exact opposite is true. All of that non-loving thinking, feeling and acting is exactly what puts them in harm's way because it weakens them and makes them vulnerable.

Most of the people in the world miss the point. They live a life that is opposite of what is good for them. They live a life of every moment hurting themselves. They doom themselves to more and more misery and suffering by being non-loving. They don't see that coming from the place of non-love is coming from a place of extreme powerlessness, extreme danger and extreme unhappiness.

Find Out For Yourself What Real Love Is.

Love doesn't need to oppose anyone or anything. Love doesn't need protection from anything or anyone. One who is being loving has the most powerful force in the universe operating their life. Negativity cannot touch one who is loving. Being loving is being powerful.

Love is the answer. Love begins with Loving Yourself.

This book shows you what real love is and how to have it. Then, it asks you to practice love. It's about practicing what I'm talking about. This book is about working along with me. This book is about learning what real love is by practicing it.

Practicing love is the easiest and simplest thing you can do. Practicing non-love is hard. Look at everyone's face and you can see that. Practicing non-love makes people sick and miserable. It robs them of their happiness and abundance.

Love is the answer.

4

Prove it to yourself. Find out for yourself what real love is. Find out where to get it and how very powerful it is. Find out for yourself how love can change your life and give you all the happiness in every area of your life.

Everyone is busy chasing love and happiness. To find it, many people work their fingers to the nub, and they die in desperation and frustration. It does not have to be that way. You can have it all. You can have all the love and happiness in the universe and everything that comes along with it. Decide to practice love. Begin with practicing it on yourself. You will learn to do that in this book.

When you love yourself, you gain everything. You do it by applying love.

When you know what love is you have the most powerful force in the universe at your disposal. Find out. Prove it to yourself.

Love yourself, and watch what happens in your life.

Love is the answer.

It's the best thing I have ever done for myself, and the finest gift I have given myself in my life. I am learning to love myself unconditionally.

— NYK, Virginia

Special note from the author:

Good things are on the way into your life.

Positive will begin to come your way as you work with what you learn in this book. Start noticing these positive happenings in your life. We call them "gains." Expect good things to begin coming into your life right away as you apply what you learn in this book. Expect unexpected gains.

As you go through the book, you will see a small sampling of thousands of gains that people all over the world, of all ages, have gotten by practicing what you will learn about in this book

Write down your gains. Pages have been included at the back of the book for you to write gains that will come as a result of applying what you learn in this book. Write down the positive things you notice happening in your life.

Writing your gains reinforces the gains. Writing gains is proclaiming positive to the universe. It's proclaiming something good has happened in your life. Writing gains is proclaiming gratitude. Writing gains opens you up to more gains.

Positive attracts positive. As you learn about love, you're going to attract many positive gifts into your life.

Your mind will say it's a coincidence. Your mind will want to minimize your gains. It will want to invalidate your gains. A gain is anything positive that comes into your experience. Notice the word "anything" positive. Anything. Let's say it another way. Any gain is a gain. Anything positive that happens in your life is a gain.

Gains are a big deal. Gains are something positive that happened to you. Positive attracts more positive. Write down your gains and you will have more and more gains to write down.

Count anything positive that happens as a gain. Write it down. Love each gain no matter how trivial it may see at the time. Any gain is a big gain. Count each and every gain. Write them down and you will have gains, a-gain and a-gain and a-gain and a-gain.

WHERE ARE YOU GOING?

I made a decision. Doubt is gone. I made a decision and it was the easiest thing to do. No going back and forth. Only, straight forward on purpose. A new quiet confidence has overcome me.

— HZ, Michigan

Who decides your direction? Is it you? Or, does it happen by default? Did you read about a man who strapped himself to a huge bundle of helium balloons? He miscalculated. The balloons carried the man much farther away than planned. He was never seen again.

How about your life? Do you have an intention for everything you do? If not, you could end up like the man with the balloons. Sailors are careful to set their sails so they reach their destination. And, you too should set your sails.

Have an intention for everything you do. Intentions are mini goals. Intentions get you where you are going. They assure that you reach your destination.

What is your intention for this book? What's your destination? What do you want to take away from this book?

Let me share my intentions with you.

My intentions for you are:

- You find out what real love is.

- You find out the "how to" of love.

- You learn to apply love and have everything you ever desired or dreamed of in your life.

- You get tools in this book to increase your capacity to love.

- You get the ways and the means to love yourself and have amazing gains.

Now it's your turn. Take a few moments and write the gains you would like to achieve from this book. Stretch your dreams. Because when you learn to apply love there are no impossibles.

_____

_____

_____

_____

_____

_____

_____

_____

I wish you a wonderful and fascinating journey to your destination.

CHAPTER ONE

YOU HAVE TWO WEEKS TO LIVE

by Larry Crane

Lester Levenson was seeking happiness just like you.

Lester went about it the same way most people do. He went to school and worked hard. To put it in his own words, Lester "battled his way through life like everyone else." Lester was looking for love in things and people. "I was banging my head so hard on the brick wall of the world," said Lester, "that I almost smashed my brains out."

Lester had ulcers, migraines, jaundice, kidney stones, and finally his second heart attack. It was his second massive heart attack, and it nearly finished him off at age 42. They didn't have all the so-called "miracle" treatments they have today. No bypass surgery, drugs, machines or all of the other things they have to save people from dying. It looked like Lester was a goner.

When he came out of the emergency room, the doctor told him, "Lester, we're sorry to tell you, but you have two weeks to live, three at most. We can't do anything for you." They sent him home to die.

"I was at the end of my rope," said Lester.

"I was told not to take a step unless I absolutely had to, because there was a possibility that I could drop dead at any moment. This was a terrible, shocking thing to suddenly be told that I couldn't be active anymore, having been so active all my life. It was a horrible thing.

"An intense fear overwhelmed me. I might drop dead any minute. After several days of this intense fear of dying, I suddenly realized, 'Well, I'm still alive. As long as I'm alive, there's hope. As long as I'm alive, maybe I can get out of this. What do I do?' I began to question, 'What am I? What is this world? What is my relationship to it? What do I want from it?'

"I saw that I wanted happiness. I asked myself, 'Well then, what is happiness?' I saw the closest thing to happiness was love. And it was a tremendous thing because I hadn't had happiness. I saw I hadn't had happiness because I always wanted to be loved. I always looked out there for people to love me. If they loved me I could be happy, I thought. I saw the happiness I got that way was very fleeting and left me back to feeling miserable and sick.

"I began to review my life. Suddenly, I got an inkling that it was when I was loving that I had the highest feeling. I saw my happiness equated to me being loving. If I could increase my loving, then I could increase my happiness."

Lester saw that the way to increase love was to let go of non-love feelings. He asked himself, "If I could get rid of all of my non-loving feelings, would I get better?" He began reviewing incidents from the past. Where he saw he was not loving toward someone, he would change that feeling to loving that person.

Months went by and Lester still wasn't dead.

He hardly slept. He ate little. He continued to work on himself. As he did, his body corrected itself. All of his miseries dropped away. He found himself in a place in which he was happy all the time. He totally cured himself. In fact, he never saw another doctor for the rest of his life.

Seeing that happiness, health, wealth, and peace of mind are determined by a person's capacity to love, was a terrific insight and gift to us from Lester Levenson. He spent the remainder of his life helping others discover this secret that he had unlocked for himself. Lester lived another 42 years after the doctors told him he had only two to three weeks to live. Before he died, Lester asked me to continue his work.

CHAPTER TWO

JUMPING FROM THE TENTH FLOOR

My name is Larry Crane. My story reached a crisis point one Friday night. I was standing on the terrace of my penthouse apartment in Manhattan, thinking of jumping.

Let me start from the beginning.

I was born in the Bronx. I grew up in a poor family. I thought the rich people lived on the top floor and the poor people lived in the basement. We lived in the basement. As a young boy, I had many, many jobs. I was very aggressive. I worked hard and put myself through New York University's Leonard Stern School of Business.

After graduation, my Father told me if I could make $100 a week it would be a terrific accomplishment. I noticed some of the friends I graduated with started to be successful and were making a lot of money. I said to myself, "I'm as smart as they are. I can do that, too." So I went about life and business in a very aggressive way, "Get out of my way. I'll take what I want. I'll have what I want or I'll knock you down." I climbed my way to the top.

I started in the advertising business. After a few very successful years, I started my own direct mail business. It was the first of its kind to sell record packages on television. The company quickly became very successful. We started to make millions of dollars. I divorced my first wife and married a beautiful, beautiful woman. I bought the fabulous ten-room duplex in Manhattan. I had limousines and planes. I had businesses all over the world. I was making many millions of dollars. Yet, I was absolutely miserable! It confused me.

Time magazine had just written an article about me. A few days later, the limo driver dropped me off at my apartment. The doorman greeted me saying, "Mr. Crane, what an honor to have you in my building. It's my pleasure to take you up to your penthouse." It was a Friday night around 9 P.M. I remember getting out of the elevator. As I entered my apartment, I felt so unhappy and miserable. I walked over to the terrace. For about two hours, I contemplated jumping and ending it all.

Fortunately, I decided not to jump.

**I call this the second greatest day of my life,
because it was a turning point for me.**

That evening, I began to examine my life like Lester did. I asked myself, "What am I doing on the planet? What is life about?" I saw that I didn't know what I was doing here. My life was only about making money. My focus was entirely on money. I didn't even allow myself to spend or enjoy much of what I made. It was confusing.

I decided that evening. I had to find an answer. After all, I had no reason to be miserable. I had millions of dollars, a beautiful wife and children. I had a fabulous business with branches all over the world. I had media attention. I had all the toys and all the trappings of what the world calls success. Still, I was miserable.

I needed to find the answers.

I wasn't into drugs or drinking. All that had no appeal to me. I wasn't receptive to psychiatric work. I wasn't open to Transcendental Meditation or yoga. I was pretty closed in those days. Yet, I had determination to find an answer. I didn't know what that answer was. I looked into some New Age classes. After taking several of them, I still found no answer that would put an end to my unhappiness.

16

I tried and I tried. I still didn't have the answer that I wanted. Getting out of my misery was all I really wanted. I discovered I was angry. I discovered I had fear. I discovered my behavior was destructive and not too intelligent. Yet, I didn't know what to do about it. None of those classes had shown me what to do about it. I became more and more frustrated.

One day, a salesman came into my office. I had some interesting spiritual and self-discipline quotations on my office wall. Those quotations often prompted conversations about the answers I was seeking. The salesman noticed the quotations and told me about "The Release Technique." It really resonated with me. I decided to take the course that very weekend. That's the weekend I met Lester Levenson.

The day I met Lester was the single greatest day of my life.

CHAPTER THREE

ALMOST NO ONE KNOWS THIS

To love yourself, to be loving, it helps to know what love really is.

Almost everybody thinks they know what love is. However, very few really do. Many people get their information about love from movies, popular song lyrics, sources like that. Many people mistake romance for love. People mistake excitement for love.

Most people look at love as a deal. They say, "If you do what I want you to do, I love you. If you don't do what I want you to do, I want you out of my life." If it sounds harsh, check it out in your own experience. People get angry with their so-called loved ones because they don't do what they want them to do. That's why the divorce courts are so busy.

Love is not what most people think it is.

Let's take a look at what love really is. Knowing what love really is helps us to be loving. In the following pages, Lester Levenson tells us about love in his own words.

Love is misunderstood. Love is a thing the world sings about, writes about, has movies about, and knows very little about. Movies portray people winning each other over. All that is human love. Human love is selfish. Divine love is completely selfless. Real love is winning the universe, not just one person but every person, every being. Real love, divine love, is a constant, persistent acceptance of all the beings in the universe.

Almost all people mistake ego approval for love. Because it is not love, it is not satisfying. Consequently, one continuously needs and demands it. And, this produces only frustration.

The best definition of love is a feeling of giving with no expectation of receiving anything for the giving. Love is giving with no strings attached.

Love is Giving.

When you are loving, you are giving. It's a very free giving. The giving may be giving of things, but it's much higher if your givingness is an attitude. Your attitude is, you want the other person to have what the other person wants. The best example is the mother who will sacrifice everything for the child without considering herself.

Most people who give are not giving lovingly. The are giving because of the recognition they think they will get from giving, 'Look at me. I'm doing good,' or 'I may get my name in the paper,' or something like that. That kind of so-called love will get you in trouble. People will drain you because you're looking for something in return. You're looking to put yourself up in the process and therefore they'll pull you down.

Love Is A Constant Attitude.

Love is an attitude that is constant. It doesn't vary.

Love is an attitude that requires no action. The love we are talking about is love you apply to everyone. You love strangers as much as you love your family, when you are being loving according to what love really is. You love those who oppose you as much as you love those who agree with you.

Love is a constant attitude that evolves in you when you develop it. You should practice love. First on your family. Try to love your family more and more. Grant each family member their own beingness, if you can. It's difficult to do, especially with children. Recognize each family member, including a child, as a whole, complete, infinite individual child of God. If you can't do it, keep trying until you can. Then apply the same attitude to friends, then strangers, then everyone.

People need each other and think it is love. The concept of possession, of holding onto, of fencing in, is the opposite of the meaning of love. The way the world looks at love is not about sharing love but about gaining personal satisfaction, fulfilling some need of the ego. Real love, the love we're talking about, wants nothing more but to share its love, and the more it is shared, the more joyous it is.

Acceptance is another good definition of love. When you love people, you accept them they way they are. You don't try to change them. You grant them their beingness. In other words, you let them be the way they want to be rather than trying to change them to be the way you want them to be.

Love has a sense of freeing those you love. When you are loving, you love the other one *because* of the way they are.

When there is full love you feel yourself as the other person. You treat the other person like your very own self.

Love is not an emotion in the sense we usually think of emotion. Emotion is energy in motion. It's an intense, active, disturbing thing. The feeling of love is the most peaceful feeling there is. In that sense, love is not an emotion.

Love is Power.

Love is a tremendous power. Mahatma Gandhi is a good example. He taught, the British are our brothers, we love the British. He taught nonresistance to the British and taught his followers to express only love for them. When you love your enemies, you have no more enemies.

To love your enemy is the height of love. Loving the enemy makes the enemy impotent, powerless to hurt you. When you really love, you can never be hurt.

Love cannot be applied to one and not another. Real love can't be turned on and off. When you're loving, it's impossible to love one person and hate another. When you love one person more than another, it's because that someone is doing something for you. That's trying to get something and that's not the love we're talking about. That is human love, not the real love we're talking about. To the degree you hate anyone, to that degree you're unable to love others. Your love is no greater than your hatred is for any one person.

Loving someone because they are nice to you is human love. It isn't the love we're talking about because if they're not nice to you then you hate them. True love is unconditional. In true love one loves even those who oppose them. Gandhi showed us how to do that and how effective that kind of love is.

Here is How to Measure Your Love.

Here is how to measure where you stand on the subject of true love. Love everyone equally. Your ability to love everyone equally is a tremendous yardstick for checking yourself and checking your growth in true love. To test your own state of love, look at your enemies. If you don't want to go that far, look at strangers. Examine your attitude toward strangers.

Your goal is equal-mindedness toward all beings, loving everyone equally. Your attitude should be: "You are me. I am you." Your attitude should be they are my family. Every mother is my mother. Every father is my father. Every child is my child. You achieve this attitude through understanding. That is the real sense of the word love. With this attitude you maintain love toward all beings; you maintain harmlessness for all beings. You maintain an attitude you want for them what they want for themselves.

One should strive to love, never to be loved. It's impossible to get love. Only by loving can you experience love. Striving to be loved can only bring temporary happiness and temporary ego inflation followed by ego deflation. When you are loving fully, there is no possibility of not being loved.

The easiest thing in the universe is to love everyone. Once you discover what love is, it's the easiest thing to do. It takes effort and agony not to love. It takes tremendous effort not to love everyone. When you love you are one with everyone. You are at peace and everything falls into line beautifully.

You get mixed up because your ego idea of love, the world's idea of love, is when you give something away you have less of whatever you give away. When you're loving there's no self sacrifice, no renunciation of your own interests in favor of the interests of others. We don't hurt ourselves when we love everyone. That's what the world thinks. But that isn't the love we're talking about.

Love is the Most Powerful Force.

It's impossible to be hurt when you love fully. You are never hurt when you love fully. You only feel wonderful when you love. In fact, you feel the greatest when you love. When you love all the time, you love every being, you have nothing but a tremendously wonderful, warm attitude of everything is fine, every person is just right. That's the way you see the world when you love. When you hate, you see the same world in just the opposite way. So, it's a tremendous thing to learn this little secret of the power of love.

Once you see what love is, the power behind love is more powerful than the hydrogen bomb. Love is the most powerful force in the universe. This love is not the love you've been taught to think it is. Love is nothing but the self with a capital "S" that is God. God is love. God is all powerful. One with God is a majority. One individual with nothing but love can stand up against the entire world because this love is so powerful.

Love will give not only all the power in the universe, it will give all the joy and all the knowledge.

Being loving, increasing your capacity to be loving, is gained by practicing being loving. As has been said, start with your family, your friends, then strangers.

By the way, the main thing a child wants from a parent is love. You can't fool a child. They know your feelings and that's what they feel. They don't listen to the words you put out. You fool yourself, you fool others with words, but you don't fool children.

But giving love to a child will develop love in that child this lifetime and will condition that child to a very happy, a most happy life.

I've always said to mothers, 'If you want to help your children, help yourself.' That's the very best way of helping your children. Before you can love a child, you have to know what love is, develop it, and be capable of loving. If you were capable of loving, instead of conflict with children, it would be the opposite, it would be a complete harmony between parent and child.

It's only because we've lost sight of what love is that we are in this difficulty of opposition between parent and child. There's hardly a family in which this doesn't exist today, it's just a matter of how little or how much it is. Because the world, as it is today, is in a very confused state, it knows very little of the real values we came here for and is lost in chasing the false god called money, prestige and so forth.

The More You Practice Love,
The More You Love.

The more you love, the more you can practice love. The more you develop your capacity to love, the more you come in touch with the harmony of the universe, the more delightful your life becomes, the more bountiful, the more everything. It starts a cycle where you spin upwards. If you want to be loved, the way to do it is to love. It's not only the best way to do it but it's the only way of receiving love, to give love, because what we give out must come back.

Being loving is easy, because right now you are all loving. You don't see it because it's smothered over by wrong attitudes, non loving attitudes, I don't like him, I don't like her, I don't like them, I don't like that group of people, I don't like that kind of people, I don't like people from that country, from that city. I don't like people from that part of town. Those attitudes are all in the direction away from love, they cover over the natural, all-loving being that you are. With all those non-love attitudes you are moving away from the loving being that you really are.

When you're non-loving, non-loving experiences come back to you and you have more and more things not to love. When you're non-loving, you have to be on guard. You have to protect yourself. If you're not loving the world, you're always protecting yourself from the world, causing more and more negative thoughts which put you on extreme defensiveness and it builds up subconsciously year after year. Then, you have a mass of negative thoughts protecting yourself from the world.

The opposite happens when you love the world. When you love the world, the world can't hurt you, your thoughts get quiet, your mind gets peaceful and then the infinite self is right there and you experience tremendous joy.

You have taken your infinite beingness, your infinite joy, and you covered it over with thoughts, thoughts of limitation. These negative thoughts smother the infinite self that you are. They smother your capacity to enjoy. All you need to do is quiet those thoughts, rid yourself of those thoughts and what's left over is the infinite, glorious being that you are, absolutely perfect and can never change.

Love is the Answer.

You are seeking love through your every act. Every human being is seeking love through their every act. If you trace through all your behavior or the behavior of people, what are they looking for? They're looking for love. That's the ultimate. That's the greatest of all progress, it's love. Our life is getting far too complex and it's not progress because people are not happier today. And, I'd say it's because of a lack of love.

Practicing love you affect every atom in the universe. You affect every person whether they realize it or not because you're invoking the power that's most powerful. It's loving every person into a perfect being.

Love is the answer to all problems. Whatever the problem is, if you just apply love to the fullest extent possible and succeed, that problem will drop immediately. Just don't get aggravated. Just know that everything is fine, everything is all right and just feel love and you'll see the problem resolve itself, no matter how difficult a problem it is. When there are problems, if you would love more they would disappear. When love is complete, any problem dissolves immediately.

The power and effect of love is obvious, just try it, apply it, and you will like it.

It's a very powerful thing, this thing called love.

Only by loving does love come to us.

The more we love, the more love comes to us.

I have gained a more peaceful and accepting outlook on life and situations. I feel more love (and only love) for everyone. Life is so much easier now!

— GC, California

I took a break from filming "Dynasty" and decided to learn how to do this. I was suffering from several stressful situations in my life. Applying these principles, I was able to get rid of frustration and anxiety. It really works!

— Joan Collins, Author and Actor

CHAPTER FOUR

HOW TO GET LOVE

Lester Levenson will show you what love is.

How do you feel about love, right now?

Here is how some people feel about love:

They like what Lester said, but they don't have love. They don't know what to do to get love. They're constantly asking themselves how to get love. They might be angry and fearful about love. They're concerned. Not being able to get love is frustrating to them. It's keeping them negative a lot of the time.

They're afraid they'll never have love. They're angry they don't have enough or maybe even any love. They feel desperate about love. It's plagued them for a long time, maybe all their life. They just want more love.

Did you notice? You felt negative as you read those words just now, didn't you? You felt negative, because all those words, all those thoughts, are negative.

Do people who *have* love say those words? Do they have all those negative feelings? Of course, they don't.

How much love is available to you, anyway? There's an infinite supply. You should have as much love as you would like to have. You should have plenty of love. You should feel love all the time. You should be able to say, "My life is full of love."

People who have love, feel they have plenty of love. They feel they have all the love that they need. If you ask them how they feel about love, they'll say, "Great," and they'll say it enthusiastically.

That's their answer to having love.

The universal law is: Positive attracts positive. Loving people have love. They have love because, they're positive about love. When it comes to love, the only thought in their mind is, they have plenty of love.

The other side of the universal law is: negative attracts negative. Negative thoughts and feelings about love leads to having more negative thoughts and feelings about love, and less and less love.

Loving people think positive thoughts about love all the time. They feel love coming their way all the time. Positive attracts positive.

The person who is struggling, searching for love and having a lot of negative thoughts about love, is pushing it away with all the negativity. They are pushing it away with the thoughts of, "I don't have it. I can't get it."

The truth is, whatever you think about all the time, is what you get more and more of all the time.

To get love, get positive about love. There's no other way. Get positive, and positive starts coming your way. That's the law of the universe. It's simple.

How do you get positive? You get positive by getting rid of negativity. Getting rid of negativity means getting rid of your non-love feelings. As you do, you begin to experience more and more love.

It takes a decision. Get rid of the negative, non-love feelings. Get positive and be loving all the time.

All the love in the universe is right there, right where you are, waiting for you to see it.

> *I never thought I could feel this good about myself. I now have a tool I can use each day of my life.*
>
> — YM, California

CHAPTER FIVE

THE MOST IMPORTANT THING YOU CAN DO

Love Yourself

Loving yourself is the easiest and smartest thing you can do. Loving yourself is also the simplest thing you can do.

Love yourself. Those two words will change your life and bring you everything you desire. Love yourself and have more happiness than you ever imagined.

Up to now, you haven't loved yourself because your mind prefers that you beat yourself up for any little thing. Check it out. Watch how many times a day your mind tells you to beat yourself up for even the smallest thing.

You can't find a parking place, so you beat yourself up. Your coffee gets cold, so you beat yourself up. You've got a pimple on your face, you beat yourself up. It happens a thousand times a day. Do you see it? You're listening to that mind of yours and beating yourself up.

How does beating yourself up help you in any way? I'm sure you agree, it doesn't. However, your mind has you convinced beating yourself up helps you. Here is what it does for you: It gives you headaches, stomach aches, back aches and body aches. That's what beating yourself up does for you. It also gives you bank account trouble and relationship problems.

Call some guy. Tell him bring a baseball bat over to your house. When he gets there, ask him to beat you over the head with the bat. Silly isn't it? That's what you're doing to yourself all day everyday when you disapprove of yourself. You might as well hit yourself in the head with a stick. No wonder you're exhausted at the end of the day. Look at what you're doing to yourself.

You're stealing your own happiness. You're stealing your own life away. That's what you're doing. Can you see it? See what you've been doing. You've spent your entire life beating yourself up. That's why sometimes you may be sick and miserable and have no energy. Decide. It does not help you, all this beating yourself up.

It's not helping you. It's not helping you get happy or healthy. It's not helping you get anything positive in your life, because it's negative.

Beating yourself up is negative, and it cannot do one positive thing for you. Decide to stop beating yourself up. It's not helping you. Decide to love yourself instead. And, decide to love yourself some more. And love yourself even more despite that mind of yours kicking and screaming.

You can turn your life around. You can feel great. You can feel the greatest. Love yourself and see.

> *I actually let go of beating myself up. I hadn't thought it was possible. I feel energetic and exhilarated after years of fatigue and depression. I have clarity and peace. I have confidence. I have a feeling of "I can" after years of feeling defeated. And, now I see it was because I was beating myself up. I'm finished with that forever.*
>
> —LUF, California

Love yourself. Try it. You'll like it. You'll like it because when you do it, you'll feel the best you've felt in years. Love yourself and you'll see your life getting better and better. Love yourself. Your life will be more and more happy.

Despite all evidence thrown at you by your mind, despite all you've ever done in your life or failed to do, love yourself. Love yourself and see what happens. No matter what your mind says, love yourself. Whatever the rest of the world is doing, love yourself.

When you spill coffee on yourself, love yourself. When your boss yells at you, love yourself. When you catch a cold, love yourself. When a notice comes in the mail from some creditor, love yourself. When your bank account is overdrawn, love yourself. When you lose your wallet, love yourself. When your spouse runs off with the neighbor, love yourself.

Whatever is happening, love yourself. And then, love yourself some more. The world may be as crazy as ever, but for you it will change. Love yourself and your world will be positive. Love yourself and your world will be happy. Love yourself and all your problems will melt away. What's left over will be the happy, loving person you have been all along covered up by the negativity.

Love yourself for just one week and see how much better you feel. It costs you nothing and it gives you everything.

Love yourself and watch love come to you. Love, and everything else you've ever wanted, will be yours when you love yourself.

It is simple. Love yourself.

CHAPTER SIX

WATCH YOUR LIFE SPIN UPWARD

Love is the most powerful force in the universe.

True love is more powerful than the hydrogen bomb.

Apply love. Love more. Any situation which you don't like, will transform if you love more. Any situation transforms into perfection when you apply love.

What does "apply love" mean? First of all, it means not to hate. That sounds easy, doesn't it? How many would raise their hands if asked if they hate? Probably not many. But if you're not loving, you're into the opposite, hating, to one degree or another.

Another word used to describe the opposite of love is disapproval. If you're disapproving of anyone or anything, the negative, disapproving energy is in you. By long practiced habit, you've gotten the idea that disapproving of yourself or others is Ok, that it does something for you. Look close and you'll see it runs you into the ditch.

A very good starting point is to love yourself. Give yourself approval all the time. Put yourself to sleep giving yourself approval and wake yourself up in the morning giving yourself approval. Your mind doesn't want you to do it. It wants you to forget. Overcome your mind's forgetfulness. You will see how giving yourself approval will turn your days and nights into a positive direction.

Apply love. Love more. To do that, first let go of non-love. Begin to give yourself approval by letting go of disapproval. You become more loving when you let go of being non-loving.

You've forgotten that you're all love. The non-loving feelings have caused you to forget that your natural state of being is all loving. You realize your lovingness when you let go of the non-loving feelings. How do you do that? It is very simple. It's just a decision. Can you let go of the non-loving feelings? Yes, you can. Let go of the non-loving feelings and discover you've been all loving all along.

Make that discovery and watch your life spin upward.

Lester often said, "I only know what I can do." Here is an example of "doing," of being loving, and how it worked.

We were under some heavy pressure at work to get system tests written for a flight control system. The pressure on us testers was great but did not compare to the pressure the designers were under. The pressure was so great that we were told not to bother the designers even for a minute to ask a question. We had to rely on half-baked documentation to write our tests for this very complex system. As a result, the project kept slipping further and further behind. Upper management replaced the System Test Project Managers every few months as one after the other would fail to bring the test activities under control.

The program resorted to bringing in a "hit-man."

The best I can describe him is that his behavior resembled the type of leadership Saddam Hussein might have had. He was very threatening, would yell and scream at us, and randomly fired several people on the spot. He demanded that we produce our tests to a virtually impossible schedule. Everyone hated him. And, it seemed he liked it that way.

"Hmmm...," I thought to myself, "What's this guy doing in my life?" What's he here to teach me?

***I decided to let go of disapproving
of him and give him approval.***

It was like he was a sponge, soaking up the love. He began to pay special attention to me in the meetings, making little jokes, and even saving a seat for me across from him. He would ask other people to move to allow me to sit down in what was now "my seat." He would even call me at my desk to come talk to him in his office. Instead of getting a verbal lashing, as I had initially expected, he would ask about my health and soon we were chatting about movies, his home country and his childhood.

He started warming up to the team and the team started warming up to him. He would even say nice things to the team and tell us how good we were doing and he was proud of us. He stayed for a few more months on the project and upper management gave him accolades for his performance in keeping the team on schedule.

When he left, we said our goodbyes, and he even hugged me.

It was truly an amazing transformation. With my conscious intention to give him approval, knowing that every living being is seeking love with their every act, he responded immediately. And his response was obvious, warm and real.

To this day, I have nothing but pure, unconditional love for this person. And, as thoughts of this man occasionally cross my consciousness, I stop for a moment and send him approval.

The power of Love is limitless. I found that out in my own experience.

— Jodi Carr, Arizona

CHAPTER SEVEN

YOUR MIND WON'T LET YOU

Resistance to loving yourself means you don't want to do it. You resist it. Resistance blocks you from moving forward. Resistance can block you from loving yourself. Resistance can block you from doing the smartest thing you can do for yourself.

Resistance can keep you stuck in non-loving and negativity. Loving yourself makes you happy, healthy and wealthy.

One sweaty summer day, a man in his 80's was hiking with much younger friends. The older man suddenly started running up a steep hill. He beckoned the younger men to join him. They ran and ran until they reached the top of the hill. When they did, the younger men doubled over. They were out of breath and in a lot of discomfort. As they caught their breath, what they saw startled them. The 80 year old man was standing there, smiling and amused. He wasn't out of breath. He wasn't breathing hard. He wasn't sweating.

The 80 year old man was Lester Levenson. As you read at the beginning of the book, Lester faced a death sentence. He saw that love is the answer. Lester found that as he let go of his non-loving, disapproval feelings, he became more and more loving. He healed his body, his pocketbook, his entire life. Lester let go of his resistance to love and lived for another 40 years sharing with others what he had learned.

What is stopping you?

You too can fly through your life like Lester raced up that hill. Resistance is stopping you. All the accumulated feelings that say, "I don't like him or her. I don't like them. I don't like it." Those feelings are negative and non-loving. They're resistance. They cause your life to be out of breath. Have you ever come home, flopped in a chair exhausted and not moved for hours? Resistance, your non-love feelings, is the cause.

All your life you've accumulated negative, non-love energy.

Ever wonder why results in your life are negative, or not as positive as they could or should be? Now you see it. Resistance keeps you stuck in non-love. Resistance blocks you from being loving and having all that the universe has to offer you.

You have *smothered* your natural, all loving, all positive, all abundant self with negative, non love feelings. You're using your positive energy to hold down all those non love feelings. Because, you don't want to deal with them. That's why you flop in the chair exhausted at the end of your day. That's why the 80 year old Lester wasn't out of breath when he got to the top of the hill.

Resistance in your mind is like a virus in your computer. Your mind works like a computer. Your computer malfunctions when you put negative programs in it. Your mental computer malfunctions if you put in negative programs called non-love feelings. Your computer turns into a pile of junk if you put too many negative programs into it. It's the same with your mind. Resistance turns your mind and your life into a pile of junk.

> *It continually gets better for me to do unfamiliar tasks. I have a lot more energy and enjoyment. I have much more peace and harmony within. I seldom have an angry outburst anymore. When I do, I recover very quickly. Even my eyesight and handwriting has improved.*
>
> — JW, Minnesota

Once you start deleting the mental viruses, your life starts to work better and better. You get rid of your resistance to being loving. You overcome accumulated resistance to love. You uncover the all loving, all happy, all abundant being that you are under the negative, non-loving feelings. Your mental computer runs according to its design. Everything in your life falls into line.

Delete your resistance to love. Open up to the loving being that you really are. The world will come your way in ways you never expected.

Are you resisting being loving? Are you resisting expressing love? Are you resisting loving yourself? Holding onto negative, non-love feelings is resisting the all loving being that you naturally are.

The world and most of its 7 billion inhabitants are not happy, not healthy, not abundant and certainly not loving. It doesn't have to be true for you. Let go of disapproval and give yourself approval. Give approval to those you have relationships with. Give approval to your bank account. Give approval to a part of your body that's bothering you.

Give yourself approval. Loving yourself is the answer. It transforms any person or situation. Love conquers all. First, to make room for the positive to shine through, let go of the negative, non-love feelings.

> *When I stopped resisting loving myself my life changed. I had increased productivity on the job. I had greater clarity of mind. I was more self-confident. I responded better to situations in my life. I was calmer in difficult situations.*
>
> — YA M.D., New York

It's a decision. Life is a decision. You can do it. You can be loving. You can let go of disapproval. You can give approval. You can give more approval. You can give even more approval. And, you can do it all the time.

Love yourself. Love everyone. It's just a decision.

CHAPTER EIGHT

THERE'S NOTHING TO IT
BUT TO DO IT.

I decided to write a book about loving yourself because it's the most important thing you can do.

Loving yourself is the most important thing you can do for yourself, your family or for the planet. Loving yourself affects every area of your life. Loving yourself affects your entire outlook on life. Loving yourself affects your finances, your health and all your relationships, especially the relationship you have with the one closest to you, yourself.

Loving yourself makes you more and more positive. As you get more and more positive, more and more positive comes into your life. Loving yourself transforms your life. Love is the most powerful force in the universe. When you love yourself, you participate in that power. There's nothing better you can do for yourself than love yourself.

When you love yourself, you are happy, healthy, successful, and full of abundance. When you love yourself, you can love everyone else. When you love yourself, you are living in the harmony of the universe and everything works perfectly all the time.

When you love yourself, you're giving yourself approval. When you're loving toward others, you're giving them approval. Giving love and giving approval is the same thing. Positive thoughts, words, and feelings, are ways of giving approval. When you like someone or something, you are giving approval. Any positive energy is approval. When you don't like someone or something you are disapproving and non-loving. Any negative energy, negative thoughts or feelings toward anyone or anything is disapproval.

Being loving attracts love with no effort. Being loving has changed my life. I will even go so far as to say, it has saved my life. There are no limits to what I can do when I am loving.

— LS, Minnesota

Practice Loving Yourself and Watch What Happens in Your Life.

Are you ready for an exercise to put this into practice?

Then, let's get started. Remember, take your time and "play along" rather than just reading the words.

I'm going to show you how to give yourself approval so you will discover what real love is and you will discover where love comes from. It does not come from outside your self. It comes from inside of you.

Rather than talking about how to love yourself and how to give yourself approval, I'm going to give you the actual experience of it.

If you're like many people new to the idea of giving themselves approval, you may be wondering exactly what does it mean, how do you do it, what's it about? People who are new to loving themselves sometimes say, "I don't get it. I don't know how to give myself approval. I don't know what you're talking about."

If you're having those questions and thoughts, it means you're subconsciously beating yourself up, disapproving of yourself. Subconscious means you don't know you're doing it. If you're not able to love yourself unconditionally, you have subconscious disapproval of yourself.

Most of the 7 billion people on the planet are disapproving of them-selves and beating themselves up, so don't feel alone. It's a nega-tive habit that we picked up a long time ago. It's such an ingrained habit that hardly anyone even realizes they're doing it. Most people are beating themselves up and disapproving of themselves all day long. That means they're living in negative energy all the time. It's no wonder the world is as dysfunctional as it is.

You're Driving Your Car with the Emergency Brake On.

That's the first thing to see. You can't give yourself approval when you're beating yourself up. It's like trying to drive your car with the emergency brake on only you don't know you have it on.

Do you have questions about the idea of giving yourself approval? Ask yourself if you know how to give yourself approval. Ask your mind.

Your mind doesn't know does it? It doesn't have a clue what I've been talking about. You ask your mind questions all the time. If your mind knew the answers, you would not have to ask, you would already know. If I ask you what street you live on, you can tell me in a second, right? If I ask you your middle name, you know. If I ask you your mother's name, you have it in an instant. Your mind knows all those answers.

You ask your mind, "How do I give myself approval?" Your mind doesn't know. It does not have the answer. If it had the answer you would not ask. You would already know.

Now asking something that doesn't know is silly, isn't it? It's like looking in an empty filing cabinet for an answer that's not there but you keep looking anyway.

When you ask your mind something, such as "How do I give myself approval?" and your mind does not have the answer, it tells you to disapprove of yourself, to beat yourself up. Have you noticed that? Your mind says something like, "You're smart. Why don't you know this? Why can't you figure it out? Why don't you have an answer? Why can't you solve this?"

Your mind says, "Beat yourself up about it."

You've seen it thousands of times. "I should know that. What's wrong with me? How could I be so dumb? Why am I so stupid? I'm such an idiot." Does all that disapproval talk ring any bells? That's what's meant by beating yourself up.

How does beating yourself up or disapproving of yourself help you? Does it get you an answer? Does it solve your problem? Does it give you a solution? Does it show you what to do about the situation? It certainly does not. Disapproving of yourself, beating yourself up, does not help you, not one little bit, ever. Do you see that?

And, who's doing it? Who is disapproving of you? You are. So, if you're doing it, if you're the one who's beating yourself up and you see that it does not help you, you need to make a decision. You can be positive and love yourself, or you can be negative and beat yourself up.

What do you decide?

I assume you decided to love yourself. That's a wise decision.

Could you let go of disapproving of yourself? Could you let go of disapproving of yourself, right now, in this moment? Go along with me. Before you can love yourself, you have to let go of all that negative, disapproval energy. To make room for love you have to let go of the non-love.

So, could you let go of disapproving of yourself? Sometimes when people are new to this they say, "Well, I'm not sure if I can let it go or not." You're not sure you can stop beating yourself up? Does it feel good? You already agreed that it does not help you in the least to beat yourself up or disapprove of yourself. Could you let go of disapproving of yourself? Just a little, since it isn't helping you.

I'm only a beginner but I saw how disapproval hurt me. As soon as I stopped disapproving of myself, I saw benefits in all aspects of my life. Money issues are resolving. I feel great. I feel a sense of clarity and well being. According to my wife, I'm a better lover too.

— GD, Pennsylvania

So, could you let go of disapproving of yourself a little more? And, could you let go of disapproving of yourself some more? And, could you let go of disapproving of yourself even more? And, could you let go of disapproving of yourself even more? And, a little more? And, could you let go of disapproving of yourself even more? And, more? And, more?

And now could you give yourself some approval? That would be a smart thing to do. Could you like yourself a little bit? Could you like yourself a little bit more? Liking yourself is approval. Loving yourself is approval.

Loving Yourself is Giving Yourself Approval.

So, could you give yourself some approval? Could you give yourself some more approval? And, could you give yourself even more approval? And, could you give yourself even more approval? And could you give yourself even more approval? And, even more?

Now, see how you feel. You feel better, don't you? When you let go of beating yourself up and disapproving of yourself you feel better. Giving yourself approval turns you more and more positive. You feel better and better every time you do it.

Giving myself and others approval is a tremendous gift and tool to heal relationships and to heal myself.

— GC, California

Try something. Think about loving yourself. Think about loving yourself or giving yourself approval. Now put your head down toward your stomach or chest. See if there is a contraction there, a clutching, an uncomfortable feeling. If there is, then subconsciously you are still disapproving of yourself.

There's no reason to beat yourself up about that. You have been disapproving of yourself for a long time and this is new to you. Go easy on yourself. Give yourself a break.

All right. So, now, get in touch with that contraction, that energy you're feeling in your stomach or your chest.

OK, good. Now, open an imaginary door right over that contraction and just allow the energy to pass through that door. And let it pass through the door some more.

And let that energy you feel pass through some more. And, more and more, and more.

Check and see how you feel now. Check the contraction. It is better isn't it? Maybe that contraction is all gone or maybe there is still more there.

Once again, think about loving yourself, giving yourself approval. See if there is a contraction in your stomach or your chest. Open up the door and just allow the energy to pass through. It wants to leave, just let it leave. And let it leave some more, and more, and more, and more and even more.

Resistance is the Unwanted Feelings You Feel.

See if you have resistance to giving yourself approval. Resistance is just a feeling. It's an "it" in your stomach or your chest. Do you feel it there? Could you just let "it" go without knowing what it is? Could you just let it go some more? Could you let "it" go some more? And could you let "it" go some more? And could you let "it" go some more? And could you let "it" go some more? And, more?

See how you feel about it now. See if you still have a contraction in your stomach or your chest. If you do, just let the energy continue to flow out through the door. And, keep the door open and just keep letting the energy leave.

Now, take a look at any more resistance you have. Have you been looking for love and approval from someone else? That is a ticket to nowhere fast.

Think of somebody you want approval from, somebody you want to like you. Take a look at them. Do they have approval? Do they like themselves? Are they happy? Chances are they are not happy and don't approve of themselves. Yet, you are expecting them to make you happy or give you approval when they don't approve of themselves. It is like going to a bankrupt bank and looking for money, except they're bankrupt. The banker says, "I would like to give you some money but I don't have any money, I'm bankrupt."

Most people don't have approval, they don't approve of themselves, they don't like themselves. We go to people and try to get approval from them when they do not have approval themselves. And, they come to us and try to get approval from us when we don't have it ourselves. Do you see the impossible situation? So what is the answer?

The answer is to love yourself. It's right inside of you.

That is where love ultimately comes from, right inside you. You have so much love inside of you covered up with all this negativity. The love is literally covered up. You're looking for love outside yourself. It is inside of you where it has always been. You haven't seen it because it is covered up by negative energy such as not liking things, not liking people, disapproving of yourself and others. That's why you don't see all the love right inside of you.

Most people are in the habit of beating themselves up. They have been doing it for years. So, it can seem hard to stop. But now you have some very valuable information. You see that beating yourself up and disapproving of yourself does not help you. It is your ego that tells you to beat yourself up. It is your ego that tells you to pour out all that negative, disapproval energy on yourself. But, you are bigger than your ego.

Say to your ego right now, "I am BIGGER than you. I am BIGGER than you. I am much BIGGER than you. Now take a walk and get lost. I don't need you anymore."

See how you feel. Chances are you feel empowered. Chances are you feel a little lighter. Chances are you feel more positive.

I always say, over and over again, "Don't believe a word I'm saying, but take it for checking." Check out for yourself what I'm telling you.

Every time you let go of disapproving of yourself, you feel more approval for yourself. It is instantaneously provable, but your mind doesn't look at what's good. It's always looking at what the problem is.

See how you feel about loving yourself again. See if you have any resistance. See if you are resisting or beating yourself up about anything. Could you let go of disapproving of yourself? And, could you let go of disapproving of yourself some more?

And could you let go of disapproving of yourself some more? And could you let go of disapproving of yourself some more? And, a little bit more? Could you let go of disapproving of yourself some more? And more?

Now could you give yourself some approval? That would be a smart decision. It's up to you. It's not up to your ego. Your ego is not your friend. So, could you give yourself some approval? Could you give yourself some more approval? Could you give yourself a little bit more approval? And, a little bit more? And, a little bit more? And, could you give yourself some more approval? And, more? And, a little bit more?

Now, see if you have any resistance coming up.

That's your ego trying to control you.

50

OK. Who is in charge? Is it you, or your ego? So, could you give yourself some approval? And, could you let go of resisting?

And, if you like the way you feel, could you allow the feeling to expand? And, could you allow that nice feeling to expand even more? Could the way you feel right now get any better? Can you let go and find out? And, could it get any better? Can you let go and find out?

And, could it get any better? Can you let go and find out? And, could it get any better? Can you let go and find out?

And, allow the feeling to expand. Take an esteem bath. Allow it to spill all over your body. And, more. And, more.

See how you feel now.

Here is what Cynthia Payne of New York, has to say about loving:

I realized I was only paying lip service to the idea of loving people.

It occurred to me, he really means it when he says, we "love" people when they're doing what we want... but we want to kill them when they don't. This was such a shock to me. I had prided myself on my ability to love and approve of people, no matter what. I realized I was just paying lip service to the idea of loving and approving of people, because in that moment, I was having the worst of thoughts about everyone who had cancelled their appointments on me that week.

I can now confront, honestly, the issue of loving people, and also, loving myself. I think of the hundreds of times a day I will inwardly curse a driver, or make fun of someone's hair, or mentally criticize someone for something. I've done this for most of my long life, and it's a program that was continuing to play, even as I told myself I was loving and approving of people and loving and approving of myself.

I realize that I can turn this around by making the decision to genuinely love and approve of people (and myself), <u>regardless</u>. I feel so fortunate to have made this discovery. However, I have to remember, the *fact I have this realization and my new awareness, doesn't automatically mean people will start doing what I want. Many will continue to cancel their appointment, and do things that would have otherwise offended me. People will always be people, but I decide to let go of disapproving of them and really genuinely love them, NO MATTER WHAT. I will include it in my daily intentions going forward and stay in love.*

So, now you have a good start on loving yourself. We will continue to explore loving yourself in the next chapter. However, re-read this chapter many times. It provides good practice in learning to love yourself.

CHAPTER NINE

REACTING IS DETRACTING

You respond to your world in three ways which I call the Three Aspects of Mind.

The first aspect of mind is the sensing aspect.

For instance, you can sense if something is hot or if it's cold. Animals have the sensing aspect, and we have it.

The second aspect of mind is the automatic recording and playback aspect of mind.

That's what your mind does. It records everything and plays it back, automatically. The recording and playback unit is the most dangerous part of the mind. It's dangerous because, it's automatic. It does not discriminate. You react automatically, without seeing what you are doing.

Human beings have the ability to record and play things back. Animals have it too. For example, if you take a baby elephant and tie its foot to a stake, its mind records that it can't move. Three years later the elephant weighs a few tons. When it was attached to the stake, it recorded it can't move. Now it still thinks it can't move if it's tied to a stake. All it would have to do is flip its leg, and it would move. The elephant is not discriminating.

Discriminating means, seeing what you are doing to yourself.

Discrimination is the third aspect of mind. Discriminating is the most the most important aspect of mind. You have the ability to discriminate. You have the ability to see things clearly. You have the ability to see what's going on, to see what you are doing to yourself.

You have the ability to see that beating yourself up does not help you in the least, it doesn't do anything for anyone on the planet, and it's hurting you. That's the ability to discriminate. When disapproval comes up — and your mind says, "When you don't get what you want, beat yourself up" — when that comes up, catch it. There it is. You see it and say, "Could I let go of disapproving of myself?" And more? And more? And, more?

This simple exercise will help you practice loving yourself.

Take out a piece of paper. At the top of the paper write the word Happy. Beside the word Happy, write Positive, Loving, Successful, and Abundant. When you're happy, you're positive. When you're positive, you're loving. When you're loving, you're successful and when you're successful, you have abundance. It's all the same energy, except we put it in different words.

On your paper, write down a few things you think you need to make you happy.

There's a story in Greek mythology where the mermaids lured the sailors to the rocks. The sailors sailed their boats over and they crashed against the rocks. That's what your mind is doing. It's promising you things. You know what I mean. "I'll be happy when I get healthy. I'll be happy when I have a nice relationship. I'll be happy when I make money." And on and on. It's not going to happen when you're negative. Nothing can happen when you're negative, only more negativity.

Your mind is ready to jump on you.

Your mind is ready to pounce on you at the drop of a hat. It's always telling you to beat yourself up. Here are some examples: Your dog just died. Your mind says, beat yourself up. Your uncle just died. Your mind says, beat yourself up. You lost some money in the stock market. Beat yourself up. Your car isn't working. Beat yourself up. You lost your watch. Beat yourself up.

Can you see what's going on? How in the world can beating yourself up fix anything? Can it get your dog back, can it get your uncle back, can it find your watch, can it get your money back? No. Beating yourself up is only digging a deeper hole for yourself.

Here's a much better way to do it. My uncle just died. Can I allow myself to be positive in spite of what happened? It's not being insensitive. There's nothing you can do about him dying. Why should you feel bad? What good does it do? Would he want you to feel bad? Do you want to feel bad? Does anybody in the world want you to feel bad? Like the elephant, we recorded these programs, and they automatically play back.

Here's a better way. My dog just died. Can I allow myself to be positive in spite of what just happened? My car broke down. Can I allow myself to be positive in spite of what happened? I lost some money. Can I allow myself to be positive in spite of what happened? That's what you need to do.

Your mind can never be satisfied.
Can you be positive in spite of what your mind is telling you?

Practice that. It's a simple exercise. Your mind is always promising. It's saying you need something to make you happy. And, that is baloney. It's totally off. It's totally off because your mind is never satisfied. Your mind tells you that you'll be happy if you get this or that, and when you get it your mind says you need more or better or different.

The answer is, be positive in spite of what you have or what's happening. That's how to be happy.

Take a look at the first item you have on your list of things to make you happy. It's a simple exercise.

Can you allow yourself to be happy in spite of what's going on? Can you allow yourself to be positive some more, and more and more? Now, see how you feel. You should be feeling positive. It's simple. Take each of the items on your list and say, "Can I allow myself to be positive in spite of what is happening?" You must stay positive no matter what because the law of the universe is, positive attracts positive and negative attracts negative. You must stay positive no matter what. When you do, things in your life turn positive.

> *I can now drop harmful, negative emotions and feelings easily and have unconditional love for myself and others all the time. Not only that, things turned around for me and I sold my house for the exact asking price I wanted, easily.*
>
> — TL, Florida

Let's go back to loving yourself, to giving yourself approval. See if you're disapproving of your mind after all of this? See if you're disapproving of your mind for telling you to be negative. Your mind eats negativity for dinner. It's waiting to pounce on you. If you're disapproving of your mind, you're building up negative energy. You're feeding the negativity more negativity, when you're disapproving.

So, could you let go of disapproving of your mind? And could you let go of disapproving of your mind some more? And could you let go of disapproving of your mind some more? And a little more? And more? And could you give your mind some approval? Positive never hurt anything. Could you give your mind some approval? Could you give your mind some more approval? And a little more? And more. And more. And could you give your mind even more approval? Now see how you feel. See if your mind quieted down. It gets noisy when you beat it up.

56

I learned the benefit of saying, "I love you" to my ego. I learned the benefit of saying, "I love you" to my mind. It's so much better than fighting with thoughts and feelings I don't like. It's how to feel good.

— KB, California

Now that we have looked at all of this, how do you feel about yourself? See if you're still disapproving of yourself for whatever reason. How does it help you? It does not. And who's doing it? You are. If you're doing it and it doesn't resolve the situation, you need to decide. I'm going to be positive and love myself or I'm going to be negative and beat myself up.

Life is just a decision. It's a decision to love yourself. It's a decision to beat yourself up. It's a decision to be rich. It's a decision to be poor. It's a decision to be healthy or to be sick. It is all a decision. Who is it that's making those decisions? It's you. You are. If you let your ego make your decisions, it's taking you right down. Like I said, check it out. What has your ego done for you so far? All its done is kept you negative by telling you to disapprove of yourself all the time.

Take a few moments to do the following exercise for approving of yourself:

Check and see if you are disapproving of yourself. Could you let go of disapproving of yourself? And could you let go of disapproving of yourself some more and some more? Could your give yourself some approval? Could you give yourself some more approval? Could you give yourself some more approval? Could you give yourself some more approval? And more. And more. And could you give yourself some more approval? And more. And more. And could you give yourself some more approval? And more. And more. And even more? Now see how you feel.

Now, could you allow that approval feeling to expand? That loving feeling, that nice, light feeling, could you allow it to expand? Could you allow it to expand some more? Could you allow it to expand some more? And a little bit more. And, could the feeling you're having right now get any better?

Could you let go and find out? And could it get any better? Could you let go and find out? And more. And more. And, more.

Now, see how you feel.

> *I have experienced wonderful benefits from using the simple method of letting go of disapproval and giving myself approval. It has brought a youthful spirit from within me that has transformed me. It has manifested physically in a more youthful appearance. At a recent family reunion, a friend commented that I seem to keep getting younger and younger. He said, "You look ageless." I have learned that loving myself puts me in a state of being in perfect harmony with body, mind and spirit.*
>
> — FH, Illinois

Now here is an exercise for approving of others:

Think of somebody you're disapproving of. Now when you're disapproving of others, you're causing yourself lots of negativity. See if you can figure out how to have a relationship with somebody you're not getting along with. Ask your friend your mind if it knows how to do it. It doesn't know. If it knew you would already be getting along with that person. So, your mind doesn't know. All it knows is, if the person doesn't do what you want them to do, beat them up, disapprove of them, send some negative energy their way, ridicule them. This is our idea of love: Do what I want you to do and I'll love you. Don't do what I want you to do and I'll have nothing to do with you. That approach isn't working for you, is it?

See if you have been disapproving of someone you haven't been able to get along with. How has disapproving of them helped your relationship? How has it helped you get along with them? How has it fixed whatever you're upset about? Of course, it hasn't helped anything. And who's doing the disapproving? Yes, you're right, you are.

So, now you have a decision to make. I'm going to be positive and send approval to this person or I'm going to disapprove of them and get nowhere fast.

I'm sure you decided to let go of disapproving of them and send them approval. That's a smart thing to do.

So, could you let go of disapproving of them? Don't do it for them. Do it for you. You're the one carrying around all that negative energy. You know it doesn't help you. So, could you let go of disapproving of them some more?

Could you let go of disapproving of them some more? And could you let go of disapproving of them some more? And a little bit more. And more. And could you let go of disapproving of them some more? And a little bit more. And a little bit more. And could you give them some approval? And again, don't do it for them. Do it for you.

Could you give them some approval? Could you give them some more approval?

Could you give them some more approval? And, a little bit more?

And a little bit more? And even more.? Now, close your eyes and see if they're not smiling at you. Of course, they are.

I had an unpleasant past with my father. Frankly, I hated him. I never told him. But, every time I thought about him it was pure hate. I got serious about these ideas because I started to see all of that hate was hurting me. For about five months, I have been practicing letting go of all that hate and sending my father love. It wasn't easy at first. I worked at it and now it's quite natural. I didn't even realize things had changed until my brother put two videos on youtube.com which showed my dad actually being nice to me. Then, one day, out of the blue, my dad called me and apologized for my childhood and told me how great I am and how much he respects me. It all happened because I sent him love instead of all those hate feelings. This is a much better way to live.

— CJ, Missouri

People think it's OK to harbor negative thoughts and feelings about other people. They think the other person doesn't know about it. I have news for you. We are all sending and receiving signals without realizing it. If you have negative thoughts and feelings about someone they know it. Don't kid yourself. They know it. You might as well go right up to them and tell them, because they know it.

If you don't like somebody, you're creating bad karma. Karma is not action. It's thoughts. If you have a negative thought toward someone, you're causing karma with them, and they're going to come back at you. Let go of disapproving of them and send them approval. Love everybody around you. Love everyone you know. You'll see how your life gets transformed.

We have so many judgments about others. If you want to see how bad it is, how many judgments you have about others, take out your address book. Those are supposed to be your friends in the address book. Yet, you'll notice your mind is judging them all over the place. "He's fat, he's tall, he's short, he's rich, he's poor, he's an idiot." All of those people, you're judging them. Have a goal: "I allow myself to love each one of them." Let go of disapproving of them and send them approval. Do it for you. You'll see how your life improves.

Love is the answer to everything.

Lester Levenson got rid of all of his non-loving feelings. Not some of them. All of them. When he did, his body was healed, his pocketbook was healed, his whole life was healed. All his relationships were healed. So, love is the answer. It's the answer to everything. Love is the answer to everything. I want you to read this many times. Practice letting go of disapproving of yourself. Practice giving yourself approval. Read it over and over again.

Practice letting go of disapproving of others and sending them approval. Because the more you love yourself, the more you love others in your life, the more you're pulling abundance toward you. The more you disapprove of yourself and others, the more you're pulling negativity toward yourself.

If you're interested in loving yourself, and being healthy, and having all the relationships you want, you need to discover where approval comes from. It comes from you. It does not come from outside yourself. It comes from you. It does not come from someone else.

Seeking love from another person is the biggest waste of your time.

Seeking love from someone is the biggest waste of your time because love has always been inside yourself. All you've got to do is get rid of the mental viruses, called disapproval, and you'll be loving all the time. Looking for love from someone else is looking for trouble. It's just going to explode in your face. If your happiness depends on someone else, all they have to do is pull the rug out from under you and you're miserable.

If your happiness comes from you, its solid, you know where happiness lies. The only one that can make you happy is you and the only one that can make you unhappy is you. Once you know that, the problem of relationships is all over. You'll never have a miserable relationship ever again. Because love is inside you.When you're loving, all problems disappear. And, you know they've disappeared, when you just don't give a hoot. Everything is perfect the way it is. Love, love, love and you can't miss.

Remember, you're just love. That's all there is to it.

Note: Chapter Fourteen contains additional exercises for experiences you may be having in your life. Spend time going over the exercises that resonate with you again and again.

When I started doing these exercises my main goal was just to feel better, just to stop being unhappy all the time. As I worked at loving myself, I noticed things were getting better in other areas of my life. I lost 35 pounds without doing any exercise. My wife lost 40 pounds. And, now I have a savings account balance of $12,000 and no more bills. My whole life has changed by using this simple skill of being loving.

— DW, Maryland

CHAPTER TEN

THREE BREAKTHROUGH ACTIONS

What I'm going to show you is not a secret.

It's not a secret but most of the 7 billion people on the planet don't know about it.

What I'm about to tell is an opportunity for a breakthrough, if you decide to do it.

What I'm about to tell you will transform everything in your life, if you do it.

You should have every single thing your heart desires. You should never, ever have to settle for less than having it all. What is it that you would like to have? Is it money? Is it health? Is it happy relationships? Is it cars, houses, boats? Whatever it is, you should have it. You can have it.

Whatever is going on in your life right now, does not matter. Do you think you have been bad? Have you been good but your luck has been bad? Have things just not worked out? Have things worked out but not to the degree you would like? Are you searching for that missing piece to the puzzle? Why don't you have all the things you long for? Why haven't your dreams come true?

Whether you have all the "things" that are supposed to make you happy or, if you're feeling as low as you can go, you have in your hands right now the answer to all that's missing in your life.

You're in the right place at the right time. How many times have you heard that? It's all about being in the right place at the right time. You are, right now, in the right place at the right time.

Maybe you have kicked yourself because you were in the right place at the right time but you didn't take advantage of it. Maybe you didn't act when you thought you should have.

Are you playing the regret game?

If you are, stop it already. Regret does not do you any good at all. It doesn't help you. It drags you down. You regret you did something or didn't do something. Notice that's a negative feeling. Some people spend their whole life living in the past, regretting. That's negative behavior that keeps you negative. All you do is build up more negative energy doing that, and you're taking yourself down.

You are, right now, in the right place at the right time. Being in the right place at the right time is half the equation. Taking action is the other and most important half of that equation. Act and let regret be a thing of the past.

Are you willing to do something different in order to have something different? Many people don't act because their mind won't let them. Most people are run by their mind. As I've said before, don't believe a word I'm saying. Check it out. Prove it to yourself.

How do you know if you're run by your negative mind? Are there things missing in your life? You shouldn't be missing anything. You should have everything you would like to have. You should have the toys, and you should have peace of mind. You should have it all. You should be happy all the time. Your negative mind tries to stop you from being happy and having it all.

Your negative mind is a "can't do" machine. It's a "can't have" machine. It's a lacking machine. Your negative mind is bent on keeping you down, keeping you from all you should have, all you deserve. Even if you have all the toys, your negative mind still tortures you all the time, day and night.

**Decide to act on what I'm about to tell you.
It will change your life, if you do it.**

Take action in spite of that mind of yours trying to block you. You're in the right place at the right time.

Please read the following sentence slowly and carefully.

Love, success, positive, health, abundance, money, peace — all of these qualities are the exact same energy.

Your mind is saying, "So what?" I told you your mind would block you.

The "so what" is this. If you get what I'm telling you, you can have everything, you can have it all.

Lester Levenson showed us the way. You let go of your non-love feelings, your disapproval, your not liking feelings—those are all negative feelings — you let them go and you become loving.

When you become loving, you become positive. When you become positive you become successful. When you become successful you have abundance of everything. You have money, you have health, and you have happy relationships.

You become loving — by letting go of the non-love feelings. When you become loving all the positive things flow your way. Positive things flow your way because all those positive things are the very same energy as love.

Do you see it? Your mind doesn't want you to see it. Your mind wants to keep you right where you've always been, which is not having the continuous joy you deserve. It's time to tell your mind to take a walk and get lost. You don't need that nay-saying mind anymore. Tell that mind of yours, "Take a walk and get lost mind. I don't need you anymore."

You are in the right place at the right time. What's needed is action.

Three Breakthrough, Life Changing Actions

Make these Three Breakthrough Actions part of your life and positive things will begin rapidly coming into your life.

These Three Breakthrough Actions will change your life and bring you what you've been missing.

Practice these Three Actions and watch what happens.

The First Breakthrough Action

Let go of your non-love feelings. Pay attention to what you're saying, thinking and doing. Watch all the time. Stay awake to what's happening. Be on the lookout all the time. When you see some non-love thought, you stop it. When you see some non-love feeling, you stop it. When you see you're taking some non-love action, you stop it.

If what you're thinking, feeling, saying or doing is negative, end it. Stop it.

If I hand you a red-hot poker you drop it in a split second, right? Non-love feelings, words, thoughts, actions, all those are hot pokers. Drop them. Non-love, not-liking, disapproval, negativity is burning up your life just like a red-hot fireplace poker burns up your hand. Drop the non-love feelings like you would drop a hot poker.

Here's the test. Is it negative? Then, it's non-loving and hurting your life. Drop it.

The Second Breakthrough Action

Hold in mind what you want. Hold in mind means what you keep in your mind. Hold in mind means the thoughts and feelings that occupy your mind all the time.

You get what you hold in mind. Whatever is occupying your mind, your thoughts and your feelings, is what you manifest in the material world. It's the law of attraction.

Positive attracts positive, negative attracts negative. Love attracts love. Non-love attracts more non-love.

Love is the same energy as positive, success, abundance, health, money, peace.

If you hold in mind "I can't," you're right, you can't. If you hold in mind "I don't have it," you're right, you don't have it and you aren't going to have it. You're holding the wrong thing in mind. You're holding in mind what you don't want.

Fake it until you make it. Stop thinking you don't have it. Hold in your mind only what you want. Prove it to yourself. Make a good effort. What do you have to lose? If I'm right you get to have everything. If I'm wrong, you're no worse off.

Here is a little hint: If it doesn't work, it's because your mind talked you out of doing it. Your mind talked you out of making a decision. Your mind talked you out of being determined and persistent. You (like everyone else on the planet) have spent your entire life collecting non-love feelings. It's likely to take some time to get all of them out. However, it's worth it because, if you work at it, if you do it, it will work. You will notice changes happening the very first week if you are persistent. Hold in mind what you want.

Here's another hint: You can easily see what you're holding in your mind. Watch what you're saying all the time. Watch what you're thinking. And, you can see what you're holding in your mind by paying attention to your feelings.

Now remember, this is not about affirmations. This is not about hanging signs around your house and car. This is about holding in mind what you want. You do that by dropping thoughts, words or feelings which express what you don't want.

The Third Breakthrough Action

Make a commitment to be positive and loving, in spite of what's happening. Decide: "I'm going to be positive and loving in spite of whatever is happening." Make that your motto.

Be positive in spite of what happens. You live your life automatically reacting with emotions you learned as a two-year-old child. You're not two years old anymore, but you're still doing the same thing. End the habit of automatically reacting. It's just a decision.

Something happens that seems to be negative. You react. You leave the present moment and you go off. Does that ever solve anything? Anger, breaking into hysteria, feeling bad because someone gave you a dirty look? Negative, non-love behavior doesn't do anything for you except make you more negative and non-loving. It never solves anything. It never helps anything. I know you see that. I know you agree with me, because you have experienced it yourself many, many times.

Make a decision. I am going to be loving and positive in spite of whatever happens.

Remember the hot poker? Begin by letting go of the hot poker called negative, non-loving reactions. Try it. Prove it to yourself. Be positive and loving in spite of whatever happens, whatever is going on, whatever they're doing or saying. Be positive and loving and watch what happens.

When you're positive and loving in spite of whatever, you're moving over to the side of love. Love conquers all. Love transforms. Love is the answer.

Adopt the Three Breakthrough Actions. Practice them. Don't listen to your mind trying to talk you out of it. You're in the right place at the right time. Take action. Be loving. Let go of the non-love feelings.

Practice the Three Breakthrough Actions:

- Let go of your non-love feelings.

- Hold in mind what you want.

- Be positive and loving in spite of whatever happens.

You will be the happiest and you will have everything.

Prove it to yourself.

> *I always thought good luck was something mysterious that happened to people for no good reason. Now I understand. Now I see that luck is loving yourself. I proved that to myself because I started having great luck. All kinds of things started falling in my lap when I started loving myself and everyone else. Now I live a life of good luck. Uncanny good things are happening for me all the time now.*
>
> — BW, Oregon

CHAPTER ELEVEN

YOUR POWER IS GREATER THAN YOU KNOW

You are powerful. Do you know that? You're powerful far beyond what you can imagine right now.

You're asking, "If I'm so powerful, why don't I feel powerful?" The reason is simple. If you're like most people, you may have given away your power. You may be giving it away every day. You don't realize you are doing it because it's a habit most people build up over a lifetime.

And what is that power that we humans give away? It's the power of love. Love, the most powerful force in the universe and the most powerful energy in the universe. You have love available to you in infinite supply. Have you given your power of love away? Look back over your life. See if you have been giving your power of love away. People give away their power by reacting automatically to what goes on in their lives. Something happens, they go into their mental computer and find the reaction they think is going to protect them. They react. Someone offends them. They react with anger. Someone threatens them. They react with fear. Someone dominates them. A lot of people react by crawling into a corner and withdrawing.

Have you been running on automatic? Do you automatically respond with negative, non-loving reactions?

Most human beings decide early on that non-love reactions protect them. Most decide right out of the womb. They smile to get those adults to do what they want. If they don't get the response they want to their smile, they use anger to get the response they want. Most people still use the same reactions they used as a baby. They're on automatic. They don't see what they are doing to themselves. Those negative, non-love reactions aren't effective. Those reactions are like turning a gun on your self. All those reactions only hurt the one doing the reacting.

Those negative reactions are giving away your power, your power of love.

Let's look at some other ways we humans give away our power.

Beating up on ourselves tops the list. Beating up on ourselves is stealing our love. It's ripping ourselves off. Watch. Pay close attention to how people beat themselves up. Watch negative words coming out of their mouths. They're beating themselves up with that talk. If other people called them some of the things they call themselves, they would call the police. It's giving away powerful love energy.

People beat up on themselves in obvious ways like the names they call themselves or the negative thoughts they think about themselves. They don't like the way they look. The don't like their body. They don't like their job. They don't like their house and on and on. Many of us have a long list of things we don't like.

Watch yourself. Make your own list of how you're beating yourself up because you don't like things about yourself or your life. Watch how you're beating yourself up because of standards you've set for yourself and you don't think you quite measure up. All of that beating yourself up is draining your energy. All of that robs you of happiness. All of that is giving away your power. All of that is making you non-loving. All of that is stealing your power of love.

Disapproval is another word for beating yourself up.

Disapproval is not-liking him or her. It's not-liking this or that. Mainly, disapproval is not-liking YOU. Disapproval is not-liking yourself. You get down on yourself. Getting down on yourself takes you down. You see it in people's faces. They scowl. They frown. It is because they are disapproving of themselves.

Here is something to notice. People see someone looking at them with a scowl on their face. They assume the person is scowling at them. "That person gave me a dirty look. It must be because I'm having a bad hair day." We personalize disapproval when the other person isn't disapproving of us at all. They are disapproving of themselves and we think they are disapproving of us. It is because we are disapproving of ourselves. You are giving away your power that way.

Uncover the love that you are so that you aren't unconsciously scowling at others. It is non-loving behavior. We get down, and we are unconsciously taking others down with us. The little baby at the supermarket glances at the scowling man, and the baby thinks he is scowling at her.

Watch all the ways you are disapproving. Disapproval demonstrates how negative attracts negative. Those of us who disapprove, have more and more to disapprove of in our life. Disapprovers attract reasons to disapprove. You've seen the type. They seem to be followed around by a dark cloud.

When you are loving, you have more and more to love in your life. You have more and more success, more and more happiness. And you have more and more abundance, when you are loving.

Another way we give away our power and get into beating ourselves up is asking our mind for answers to questions. Asking our mind is trying figure something out. It's wrestling around with our mind, trying to come up with an answer. That's how almost everyone lives. That's why people are sick and miserable and non-loving. Please, for your own good, try to see this. When you ask your mind a question such as, "How do I resolve this situation?" you have taken the road into figuring it out. You know the name of the street you live on. You know your middle name. Your mind knows those answers. However, when you don't know something, it means simply that your mind does not know. If your mind knew, you wouldn't be asking.

Watch this subtlety happening in your life all the time. You don't know something. You ask your mind. You start thinking about it. You start trying to figure out the answer. You may even lose several nights of sleep tossing and turning trying to find an answer in your mind.

Your mind does not know the answers. How can you be sure? Because, you don't know. You don't have your answer or solution. It's silly isn't it? Hour after hour, day after day, year after year for all our lives, we're asking something that doesn't know. It's like looking in an empty file cabinet for an answer that's not there but we keep looking anyway. We're giving our power to that empty filing cabinet. We are giving away our love to that mind of ours. That's why a lot of the time we wake up in the morning exhausted.

When you ask your mind, it doesn't know, but it does tell you something. It tells you to beat yourself up. It tells you to beat yourself up for not having an answer, not being able to figure it out, not being able to resolve some situation.

Right this very moment, it's possible you've been looking for some answer: How to solve a money or financial issue; how to resolve a relationship issue; how to solve a health issue; how to lose weight; how to overcome stress; how to get a good night's sleep. All of that is getting you further and further into negativity because your mind has you beating yourself up for not being able to get an answer. All of that is giving up your power.

You want to be happy, so stop asking your mind and stop beating yourself up. If you want to have your power, rather than giving it away all the time day and night, stop asking your mind for answers it does not have. Get to the place where you don't beat yourself up anymore for any reason whatsoever.

Another way we give away our power is trying to get others to love us. We'll do anything to get their love. Blowing in their ear, making nice so they'll love us, is giving away our power big time. They don't love themselves. How can they love you? It's like going to bankrupt bank and trying to get money.

You're begging them to love you, but they don't have love to give you. They want someone to love them as much as you want someone to love you. Your mind does not want you to see it. Your mind wants to keep you right where you are, giving away your power of love by thinking you have to get love from someone other than yourself.

I often say, wanting approval is the biggest check you will ever write. It's the biggest check you will ever write because, it is giving away your power to someone out there hoping to get something in return, called love, and they don't have it to give to you. It's the biggest check you will ever write because, you are giving away all of your power, wanting someone to give you what you already have.

Watch the ways you are trying to get approval from people. You give away your power wanting them to like you, wanting them to love you. Wanting approval takes you down. It drains your battery. You do not need anyone's approval. You have all the love in the universe right inside of you. Let go of wanting them to like you, to love you. Instead, just love them. Just give them love, with no expectation of anything in return.

Here are a few more examples of how we humans give up our power: Getting annoyed, getting frustrated, getting outraged, getting jealous, panicking, regretting, doubting, complaining, getting defensive, dramatizing, playing the victim, worrying, and fearing. The list could go on, but better yet, watch what is happening in your life and notice your automatic negative reactions. Those negative reactions are giving away your power, your love. They're putting you on the side of being non-loving and they're draining your powerful energy.

Say to yourself, "How does this negative reaction help me? How does this make me more loving? How does this make me more positive? How does this make me feel more powerful? How does this make me more energized?" You immediately see it does not. Seeing that it does not help you, makes it easy to start letting go of power-robbing, love-robbing behaviors. It's important. Your life depends on it. Your quality of life depends on you seeing yourself doing these things, seeing that they don't help you, and taking back your power by letting them go.

Find out where love is. Love is in you, covered up by negative, non-love feelings. Regain your power. Find out. All the love in the universe is in you. Stop looking for it out there. Stop giving up your power looking for love out there.

In the next chapter, I'll show you how to regain your power, how to amp-up and get back all that power you have given up.

CHAPTER TWELVE

POWERING UP

In the previous chapter, you saw some of the ways you might be practicing non-love behavior and giving up your power.

The way to amp-up your love and reclaim your power is simple. Love yourself. That's it. That's all you have to do to regain all your power you have given up by being non-loving. Love yourself.

Start by looking for your non-love feelings all the time and dropping them. Get your power back by letting go of all those non-love feelings and loving yourself.

Life is a decision. You decide your life. You decide to be non-loving. Or, you decide that you've had enough of the misery of that kind of living, and you decide to be loving. Decide to end the life of non-love that you've led up to now. It is just a decision that enough is enough: "I am going to be loving. I'm going to love myself."

Are you ready to power up? Powering up means, all day, all the time, you use three words: "I love you." That's how you power up and regain your power. That's how you live the wonderful, positive life you're meant to have.

> *By sending love and approval, I have had many gains. I got rid of anxiety, guilt and fear I had been holding onto for years. My relationship has improved with my wife and daughter. And, the chronic pain in my neck and back is completely gone.*
>
> — JM, South Carolina

Check and see if you have been asking your mind about all of this. Check and see if you have been asking your mind how you can regain your power and be loving all the time?

If you ask your mind, you will find it does not know those answers. Your mind has no clue about being loving. Your mind has no clue how you can love yourself. It is focused on being non-loving and getting you to beat yourself up.

So, asking your mind for answers about loving yourself is silly because your mind does not know. It's like looking for an answer in a file cabinet that is empty, but you keep looking anyway. Can you see how silly that is?

Your mind has told you to beat yourself up and disapprove of yourself hasn't it? "I'm not good enough. I'm not getting it. I'm not sure about it." Those thoughts are telling you to beat yourself up.

Does all that beating yourself up and disapproving of yourself help you? Does it make you more loving? Does it make you happier? Of course, it does not. Beating yourself up does nothing positive for you. Do you see that? Sure you do.

And who's doing it? Who is beating yourself up? You are. That's right.

If it doesn't help you to beat yourself up and you're the one doing it, you have a decision to make. You can decide to be positive and love yourself or decide to be negative and beat yourself up. What's your decision? Of course, you decided to be positive and loving.

So, can you let go of beating yourself up? Drop it like the red-hot poker it is, damaging your life as it does.

It's just a decision. Can you let go of disapproving of yourself some more? And even more?

Now, since you decided to be positive and love yourself, can you give yourself some approval? Can you like yourself just a little bit? Can you like yourself just a little bit more? Can you give yourself some more approval? Can you give yourself some more approval? And more? And even more?

Now check. How do you feel? You feel better, right?

When you let go of disapproving of yourself and give yourself approval you always feel better. You feel better because you are moving in the direction of positive. You are moving in the direction of love and you are regaining your power. You become more and more loving and regain more and more of your power as you give yourself more and more approval.

> *I have been able to be at peace with myself. I can talk to people with ease now because I have more confidence in myself.*
>
> — PH, Texas (age 14)

Your mind isn't interested in you giving yourself approval. When you are giving yourself approval, your mind might even jump in and remind you of reasons you should beat yourself up. But now that you've gained some insight into how your mind works, you can just tell it to take a walk and get lost. You can continue to let go of the disapproval, let go of beating yourself up, and continue to give yourself approval.

Once you have spent time doing this you'll be glad when your mind jumps in and tells you to beat yourself up. You'll smile and say, "There you are again mind." You'll be glad because that mind of yours is pointing out to you some more disapproval that you can let go of.

And for each bit of disapproval you let go of, you reveal more love and more of your positive, loving nature. So, just let go of the disapproval and more and more and more, then go back to giving yourself love and approval, to loving yourself.

I dropped self-hatred and it was like dropping a heavy weight I had been carrying around for years.

— RK, Idaho

The more you practice letting go of beating yourself up and giving yourself approval, the more and more loving you will see yourself becoming, and the more power you will recapture. As you give yourself approval, you will see yourself becoming more powerful and moving up into a higher and higher energy.

Amp-up your power of love. It is easy. Just love yourself.

Here is an assignment: Sit down and give yourself approval for as long as you can. Increase the length of time each time you do the exercise.

Does that exercise sound foreign to you? Sure it does. But isn't it time to try something different? To have something different you have to do something different. Isn't it time to stop listening to that mind of yours telling you to beat yourself up? Isn't it time for you to take over? It's your mind. You're the owner. Isn't it time to start acting like the owner? Isn't it time to tell that ego of yours to take a walk and get lost? You definitely don't need it anymore.

May I suggest you make a decision? Decide to stop beating yourself up. Do the smartest thing you can do. Love yourself.

So switch off that TV for a few minutes. Use that time to review your day and notice when you were beating yourself up or disapproving of yourself. Let go of disapproving of yourself and let go of it some more until you can then give yourself approval. Keep giving yourself more and more approval. I love you. I love you. I love you. I love you. I love you.

You can love yourself anywhere, anytime. You can love yourself at a traffic light. You can love yourself in the supermarket check out line. You can love yourself all day long. Rather than idle time, you can use all those moments for amping-up your love, amping-up your power.

Practice loving yourself, and you will make a magnificent discovery. You are a loving being. You are love. You have love. You have access to the unlimited supply of love, the unlimited supply of love that is more powerful than the hydrogen bomb. You have that power inside of you right now covered up by the non-love, beating yourself up and disapproval feelings.

Discover yourself. Love yourself and find out. Love yourself and you will be happy, and healthy, and successful and abundant.

Love is the answer. Power up. Let go of the non-love feelings and find out. Love yourself.

The very best gift I can give myself is giving myself approval, to be loving of myself.

— LR, Wisconsin

CHAPTER THIRTEEN

PRACTICE ON YOUR KIDS

Following are the Words of Lester Levenson:

Practice love.

First on your family. Try to love your family more and more. Grant each family member their own beingness, if you can. It's difficult to do especially with children. Recognize each family member, including a child, as a whole, complete, infinite, individual child of God. If you can't do it, keep trying until you can.

People need each other and think it is love. The concept of possession, of holding onto, of fencing in, is the opposite of the meaning of love. The way the world looks at love is not about sharing love but about gaining personal satisfaction, fulfilling some need of the ego. Real love, the love we're talking about, wants nothing more but to share its love and the more it is shared the more joyous it is.

Acceptance is another good definition of love. When you love people, you accept them they way they are. You don't try to change them. You grant them their beingness. In other words, you let them be the way they want to be rather than trying to change them to be the way you want them to be. Love has a sense of freeing those you love. When you are loving, you love the other one because of the way they are.

The main thing a child wants from a parent is love. You can't fool a child. They know your feelings and that's what they feel. They don't listen to the words you put out. You fool yourself, you fool others with words, but you don't fool children. But giving love to a child will develop love in that child this lifetime and will condition that child to a very happy, a most happy life.

I've always said to mothers, 'If you want to help your children, help yourself.' That's the very best way of helping your children. Before you can love a child, you have to know what love is, develop it, and be capable of loving. If you were capable of loving, instead of conflict with children, it would be the opposite, it would be a complete harmony between parent and child. It's only because we've lost sight of what love is that we are in this difficulty of opposition between parent and child. There's hardly a family in which this doesn't exist today, it's just a matter of how little or how much it is. Because the world, as it is today, is in a very confused state, knows very little of the real values we came here for and is lost in chasing the false god money, prestige and so forth.

The best thing you can do for children is to set an example. That's the very best way to teach children, by example. They want to be like their parents. So, it always comes back to the parents. If you want to help your children you must help yourself. Then you'll find out you don't have to consciously do anything. Just help yourself and you'll see them grow.

If we love our children, we free them. We allow them to grow, to bloom, to come out like a flower does. We don't try to fence them in. We free them and guide them and love them, unattached to them, knowing they are God's beings. They are just as much God as I am, is how you should feel. Also, they are going to go through life just the way they have set it out anyway. You should strive to free them, to feel non-attached. This is a higher love than a love with attachment.

Guide them. They'll ask you for guidance if you just free them. But they resent being dominated and dictated to the same way you do, the same way you did when you were a child. They don't like to be ordered around.

But they want to learn. They have a natural curiosity. They'll ask you. If you start from the beginning by freeing them the first day, bringing up a child is one of the easiest things to do. They'll follow you. But when you start telling them from the first day what to do and what not to do, they behave like an adult does when told what to do and what not to do. They resent it. They oppose it. Then, oppositional patterns are set up and by the time the child is able to walk around, they've got this oppositional pattern well developed. That's what makes bringing up children so difficult.

Because of all our attachment to them we're trying to steer them and they resist. We were trained that way. We train our children that way and they will train their children that way and it goes on and on.

Training could be accomplished without opposition if it starts right. Show them the possibilities, the alternatives, and let them make the decisions. Then they're working with you from the beginning and they don't develop oppositional habits.

The first place to practice love is at home with the family. We should try to love our family more and more by granting them their right to be the way they are, more and more.

The main thing the child wants from us is love and we cannot fool a child. Children know our feelings and that is what they read. We fool ourselves with words but we don't fool them.

Giving unselfish love to a child will develop unselfish love in that child this lifetime and will condition the child for a most happy life.

It doesn't matter how we act as long as the feeling within is love. The attitude is more important than the act. Use this with the family.

If we were capable of selflessly loving, instead of conflict with children, there would be complete harmony. But it is only because we have lost sight of what selfless love is that we are in this difficulty of opposition between parent and child.

My relationship with my teenage son has improved tremendously. It has turned into loving acceptance of one another.

— MG, California

The following story shows how our feelings affect our experience:

One day, at the dinner table, my daughters were complimenting the food. "Oh it's so delicious Mommy, it's very good," and in no time the bowls were empty. I was very much surprised because it was not their favorite dish. So, I asked again if they really liked the food. "Yes, Mommy, it's very delicious. Make it again."

I thought about it. That day I had been feeling very good. I realized that while I prepared the food, I had very positive, loving thoughts. Those loving thoughts affected the food, which turned out very delicious.

One day, the next week, I prepared the children's favorite dish and they picked at the food. So, I asked, "What's wrong?" "Mommy, it's tasteless," they replied. What they said once again surprised me. I prepared it the same way I do every time.

I reflected and realized, while I was cooking, I had a lot of negative, resentful thoughts on my mind. I hadn't been happy as I was preparing the food.

The children taught me a lesson. I decided to be more observant and aware of my feelings and thoughts. I found out love increases enjoy-

ment. Negative thoughts and feelings affect everything in our life negatively.

— Manisha Mehta, New Jersey

My youngest son told me he loved me on the phone. It was his second phrase. He is 1 ½ years old. My oldest son stopped a bully at school using the technique of silently saying, "I love you."

— AW, U.K.

CHAPTER FOURTEEN

EXERCISES TO PRACTICE LOVING YOURSELF

With loving myself I have gotten rid of severe depression. I have gotten rid of health problems such as anxiety attacks, rapid heartbeat, colds, and even sprained ankles. Better yet, I keep feeling happier and lighter.

— AW, California

Begin Each Day This Way.

When you wake up in the morning, as soon as you open your eyes, ask yourself, "Am I disapproving of anything right now?" Let go of any disapproval. Then, give yourself approval. And, give yourself more approval and keep giving yourself approval.

Make a decision. Have the intention: "All day long I am looking for disapproval of myself. I am immediately letting it go and giving myself approval and giving myself more and more approval."

For example, how do you spend your time at a traffic light? It's another great time to look for any disapproval and let it go. Then give yourself approval and more and more approval until the light turns green. Watch how much better your day goes when you take a minute or a few minutes, as often as possible throughout the day, to let go of disapproval and give yourself approval.

I experienced the power of love. I experienced the power of saying, "I love you," especially when I don't feel like it. It really works for me.

— BW,Illinois

During your day, if you've gotten irritated, frustrated, annoyed, or some other negative feeling has taken you over, it's time to take a few minutes to notice you are probably disapproving of someone or something — maybe yourself — see that, and let it go. Let the negativity go and give yourself approval or give approval to whatever or whoever was bothering you. Remember, it doesn't help you to hold on to that negative energy, does it? You can decide, "I'm going to be positive, I'm going to let go of disapproving and give approval."

End Each Day This Way

Now that I give myself approval when I go to bed, I find I am sleeping better, needing less sleep. If I wake up in the middle of the night, I wake up to saying "I love you", which is kind of cool to wake up to that. I feel like a different person.

— CW, Colorado

Follow this procedure and you too will sleep better than you ever have in your life. Each night, as soon as your head hits the pillow, look to see if you are trying to figure anything out about what happened during your day. Let go of any figuring it out about anything. Then, check. Look and see if you have any disapproval about anyone or anything. Let go of the disapproval. And, begin giving yourself approval. Yes. Give yourself an esteem bath. Put yourself asleep giving yourself approval and you will have never slept better in your life.

After years of insomnia, I am no longer worried about sleeping. I sleep well and deeply. I feel confident because I am giving myself approval right before I sleep.

— PZ, Los Angeles

During your day if you get swept away by the negativity, it may seem difficult to be positive. But as soon as you notice the negativity, recognize that you have been saying "No" to what you are feeling. You don't like what is going on, you have been saying "No" to it. Saying "No" does not get you positive, does it? Instead, decide to be positive by saying "Yes" to whatever feeling you have. Say Yes, and keep saying Yes. Soon, the negative feeling leaves and you let go of any disapproval you may have and give approval. Then you can go on with your day feeling happier and lighter. Use this Power of Yes and there is no reason to have stress or frustration in your life. It's just a decision. Decide to be positive. By deciding to be positive, you move in the direction of happiness, abundance, health and peace. Try it. You'll like it. The next section gives you practice with the Power of Yes.

THE POWER OF YES

The following exercises are divided into categories, so you can start with the feeling that resonates most with you now and come back to this section often. The exercises are meant to be used over and over again until they are natural to you. They are very simple and extremely effective. In order to get the most from these exercises, make sure that you focus, participate, and "play along" by answering back as if I'm asking you the questions. If you do this, rather than just read these as you would other reading material, you will see the improvements in yourself in every way. Enjoy.

My 89-year-old mother suffered a major heart attack. She was home and recuperating but frustrated because of not bouncing back like she thinks she should. So, I had her say "Yes" to the heart attack and her feelings instead of saying

"No." Two days later, what a remarkable change. She has been able to get out of the house and attend a senior citizen meeting as well as go shopping with my brother. She is amazed at the difference and so am I.

— CC, Indiana

FRUSTRATION

Have you ever experienced frustration in your life? Maybe you are frustrated right now about something that has not been working for you in your life. But the question is, "How does being frustrated help you solve what's going on? " It doesn't at all! Then why continue doing it?

Would you like to have a simple exercise you can use to eliminate your frustration quickly and easily on the spot? Yes?

Ok, so think of something that frustrates you.

Now, on a scale from 1 to 10, with 10 being the most frustrated and 1 being the least frustrated, where are you right now with regard to the frustration?

I can show you a way to get rid of that frustration if you are willing to do something different. Are you willing to do something different?

Can you see that you have been saying "No" to the frustration? You don't like the frustration, do you? You have been saying "No" to it, right? But when you say "No" to it, you're actually collecting it.

So now can you say "Yes" to the frustration so that you can get rid of it? Can you say "Yes" to the frustration some more? And more? And even more? And can you say "Yes" to it again? And "Yes" again? And can you say "Yes" to the frustration even more? And more? And even more?

Now take a check. On the scale from 1-10, where are you now with regard to the frustration?

Notice that saying "Yes" to it actually lowers your amount of frustration.

Now that your frustration is lower on the scale, you have an indication that you are headed in the right direction. Saying "Yes" to the frustration allows you to get rid of it, while saying "No" to it was only collecting the frustration.

So now instead of pushing down on it, can you just invite it up? Can you say "Yes" to the remaining frustration and just let it come up and out?

Continue repeating this exercise on the frustration until you are at zero on the scale with regard to the frustration. If you were bitten by a poisonous snake, you would want to remove all the poison, not just some of it.

Holding onto frustration gets in the way of you accomplishing anything, including loving yourself. If you have frustration about a person or situation, guess who gets to feel it and carry it around? You do! So the smart thing is to bring up all your frustration and allow it all to leave so you can be happier, healthier, wealthier, and have better relationships.

> *My frustration level is way down using this method. Our business is up 40%, over a million dollars, since last year.*
>
> — BL, West Virginia

> *I practiced saying, "Yes, Yes, Yes, I love you, I love you, I love you, silently, over and over, to a co-worker who had been bothering me. Several times when thoughts of punching his lights out came up, I dropped disapproving of him and went back to saying, "Yes" and "I love you." When I returned to work on Tuesday, he and I exchanged polite morning greetings without a hint of ill-will. Since then, he no longer bothers me.*
>
> — EK, Seattle

WORRY

*H*ave you ever tried to worry your way out of a problem? Then you may have noticed that *worry has never solved a single problem, ever!* Holding onto worry only drags you further down into the problem. When you let go of the worry you are letting go of a *barrier* to the problem being solved.

Are you ready to clear out your worry and watch your problems disappear? Yes?

> ***Less and less worry has given me more and more peace.***
>
> — WL, Florida

Then think of something that you have been worrying about.

Now on a scale from 1 to 10, with 10 being the most worried and 1 being the least, where are you right now with regard to the worry?

I can show you a way to get rid of that worry if you are willing to do something different. Are you willing to do something different?

Can you see that you have been saying "No" to the worry? You don't like the worry, do you? You have been saying "No" to it, right? But when you say "No" to it, you're actually collecting it.

So now can you say "Yes" to the worry so that you can get rid of it? Can you say "Yes" to the worry some more? And more? And even more? And can you say "Yes" to it again? And "Yes" again? And can you say "Yes" to that worry even more? And more? And even more?

Now take a check. On the scale from 1-10, where are you now with regard to the worry?

Notice that saying "Yes" to it actually lowers your amount of worry. Now that your worry is lower on the scale, you have an indication that you are headed in the right direction. Saying "Yes" to the worry allows you to get rid of it, while saying "No" to it was only collecting the worry.

So now instead of pushing down on it, can you just invite it up? Can you say "Yes" to the remaining worry and just let it come up and out? Can you pull your shoulders back and allow all the worry to just fly right out?

Continue repeating this exercise on the worry until you are at zero on the scale with regard to the worry. If you were bitten by a poisonous snake, you would want to remove all the poison, not just some of it. Holding onto worry prevents you from having a solution. So when you let go of the worry, you are able to move forward and have solutions.

> *"I felt a dramatic reduction in anxiety coupled with a tremendous increase in positive energy. My blood pressure is normal after years of worrying about it and trying everything."*
>
> — TC, California

GUILT

If you hold onto or carry around feelings of guilt, you are punishing yourself. Feeling guilty interferes with your happiness and results in you holding good things away from yourself, subconsciously.

Since having this guilt doesn't help you, are you ready to quickly and easily rid yourself of guilt? Yes?

So think of something that you have been feeling guilty about.

Now on a scale from 1 to 10, with 10 being the most guilty and 1 being the least guilty, where are you right now with regard to the guilt?

I can show you a way to get rid of that guilt if you are willing to do something different. Are you willing to do something different?

Can you see that you have been saying "No" to the guilt? You don't like the guilt, do you? You have been saying "No" to it, right? But when you say "No" to it, you're actually collecting it. So now can you say "Yes" to the guilt so that you can get rid of it? Can you say "Yes" to the guilt some more? And more? And even more? And can you say "Yes" to it again? And "Yes" again? And can you say "Yes" to that guilt even more? And more? And even more?

Now take a check. On the scale from 1-10, where are you now with regard to the guilt? Notice that saying "Yes" to it actually lowers your amount of guilt. Now that your guilt is lower on the scale, you have an indication that you are headed in the right direction. Saying "Yes" to the guilt allows you to get rid of it, while saying "No" to it was only collecting the guilt.

So now instead of pushing down on it, can you just invite it up? Can you say "Yes" to the remaining guilt and just let it come up and out?

Continue repeating this exercise on the guilt until you are at zero on the scale with regard to the guilt. If you were bitten by a poisonous snake, you would want to remove all the poison, not just some of it. Letting go of all the guilt moves you more into loving yourself and clears the way for abundance in all areas of your life.

> *I started saying, "Yes" to my guilt I held onto about my mother's hospitalization and death. I kept saying, "Yes," over and over to the guilt. The guilt quieted, and now I see I did the best I could at the time. I saw I was trying to hold onto her with all that guilt. I have sent her love and approval. It was very freeing for me to drop the guilt, and I am sure it was freeing for her too, for me to finally let her go.*
>
> — FD, Colorado

SADNESS

Does staying sad about something, change what happened? Of course, it does not. And how do you feel when you hold onto that feeling of sadness? Chances are it feels pretty lousy.

So if it feels bad and it doesn't improve or change the situation at all, are you ready to free yourself from the weight of that sadness?

Think of something that you have been feeling sad about.

Now on a scale from 1 to 10, with 10 being the most sad and 1 being the least sad, where are you right now with regard to the sadness?

I can show you a way to get rid of that sadness if you are willing to do something different. Are you willing to do something different?

Can you see that you have been saying "No" to the sadness? You don't like the sadness, do you? You have been saying "No" to it, right? But when you say "No" to it, you're actually collecting it. So now can you say "Yes" to the sadness so that you can get rid of it? Can you say "Yes" to the sadness some more? And more? And even more? And can you say "Yes" to it again? And "Yes" again? And can you say "Yes" to that sadness even more?

Now take a check. On a scale from 1-10, where are you now with regard to the sadness? Notice that saying "Yes" to it actually lowers your amount of sadness. Now that your sadness is lower on the scale, you have an indication that you are headed in the right direction. Saying "Yes" to the sadness allows you to get rid of it, while saying "No" to it was only collecting the sadness.

So now instead of pushing down on it, can you just invite it up? Could you say "Yes" to the remaining sadness and just let it come up and out?

Continue repeating this exercise on the sadness until you are at zero on the scale with regard to the sadness. You can use this exercise any time and live a life free from sadness.

With my Mom's living situation and her condition, in the nursing home, and in last stages of Alzheimer's, I was having tons of grief come up, despair over her condition and care. I was feeling sorrow, pity, guilt, all of it. Now I am able to truly feel love for her, without the pain and agony that I used to have.

— PM, California

I have alleviated a deep grief I carried around for several years. I used to cry every morning. Now, that no longer happens. Now that I've let go of the grief and sadness, I have also had financial gains where money showed up in unexpected ways to the tune of over one million dollars!

— MG, California

STRESS

Most people are trying to suppress their negativity. When you try to suppress your negativity, you actually end up collecting it and then it stays there, interfering with your health, happiness, wealth, and relationships. And we call that stress.

Are you ready to rid yourself of stress on the spot, quickly and easily?

So, think of something that you have been feeling stressed about.

Now on a scale from 1 to 10, with 10 being the most stressed and 1 being the least stressed, where are you right now with regard to the stress?

I can show you a way to get rid of that stress if you are willing to do something different. Are you willing to do something different?

Can you see that you have been saying "No" to the stressed feeling? You don't like the stress, do you? You have been saying "No" to it, right? But when you say "No" to it, you're actually collecting it. Can you say "Yes" to the stress some more? And more? And even more? And can you say "Yes" to it again? And "Yes" again? And can you say "Yes" to that stress even more?

Now take a check. On the scale from 1-10, where are you now with regard to the stress? Notice that saying "Yes" to it actually lowers your amount of stress. Now that your stress is lower on the scale, you have an indication that you are headed in the right direction. Saying "Yes" to the stress allows you to get rid of it, while saying "No" to it was only collecting the stress.

So now instead of pushing down on it, can you just invite it up? Can you say "Yes" to the remaining stress and just let it come up and out?

Continue repeating this exercise on the stress until you are at zero on the scale with regard to the stress. If you were bitten by a poisonous snake, you would want to remove all the poison, not just some of it. When you let go of your suppressed negativity and stress, your life improves in every way.

> *I had been feeling real bad and been stressed-out for three months. I stopped beating myself up. I feel more relaxed, calm , less afraid and lighter now. I feel loving of myself and others.*
>
> — AS, Spain

CONFUSION

Is it possible to solve anything when you are in confusion about it? Of course, not. Confusion is a state of having no answers and keeps us from moving forward. In order to move forward into a state of clarity, having answers, and solutions, you must move out of the confusion.

Fortunately, it is simple and easy to let go of the confusion. Are you ready?

Think of something that you have been feeling confused about.

Now on a scale from 1 to 10, with 10 being the most confused and 1 being the least confused, where are you right now with regard to how much confusion you feel?

I can show you a way to get out of the confusion if you are willing to do something different. Are you willing to do something different?

Can you see that you have been saying "No" to the confusion? You don't like the confusion, do you? You have been saying "No" to it, right? But when you say "No" to it, you're actually collecting it.

So now can you say "Yes" to the confusion so that you can get rid of it? Can you say "Yes" to the confusion some more? And more? And even more? And can you say "Yes" to it again? And "Yes" again? And can you say "Yes" to that confusion even more? Now take a check. On the scale from 1-10, where are you now with regard to the confusion?

Notice that saying "Yes" to it actually lowers your amount of confusion. Now that your confusion is lower on the scale, you have an indication that you are headed in the right direction. Saying "Yes" to the confusion allows you to get rid of it, while saying "No" to it was only collecting the confusion.

So now instead of pushing down on it, can you just invite it up? Can you say "Yes" to the remaining confusion and just let it come up and out? You don't need it anymore, do you?

Continue repeating this exercise on the confusion until you are at zero on the scale with regard to the confusion. When you let go of all the confusion you are left with clarity, answers, solutions, and you are able to move forward in a positive way.

> *I was constantly spinning around getting more confused.*
> *Now, I've been saying "Yes," and I'm getting more clear and*
> *more and more at peace every day.*
>
> — ES, Tennessee

FEAR

Holding a fear about something actually creates the very thing you fear. When you hold onto the fear, you are holding in mind (so then creat-

100

ing) what you fear. Then why would anyone hold onto fear? Most of the time they think they are protecting themselves with the fear. But trying to protect yourself with fear is just like jumping in a swimming pool with a bag a cement expecting it to help you float.

Are you ready to find out how to live fearlessly?

Think of something that you have a fear about.

Now on a scale from 1 to 10, with 10 being the most fearful and 1 being the least fearful, where are you right now with regard to how much fear you feel?

I can show you a way to get rid of the fear if you are willing to do something different.

Are you willing to do something different?

Can you see you have been saying "No" to the fear? You don't like the fear, do you? You have been saying "No" to it, right? But when you say "No" to it, you're actually collecting it.

So now can you say "Yes" to the fear so that you can get rid of it? Can you say "Yes" to the fear some more? And more? And even more? And can you say "Yes" to it again? And "Yes" again? And can you say "Yes" to that fear even more? And more? And even more?

Now take a check. On the scale from 1-10, where are you now with regard to the fear? Notice that saying "Yes" to it actually lowers your amount of fear.

Now that your fear is lower on the scale, you have an indication that you are headed in the right direction. Saying "Yes" to the fear allows you to get rid of it, while saying "No" to it was only collecting the fear.

So now instead of pushing down on it, can you just invite it up? Can you say "Yes" to the remaining fear and just let it come up and out? Can you pull your shoulders back and allow the fear to come shooting right out? You don't need it anymore, do you?

Continue repeating this exercise on the fear until you are at zero on the scale with regard to the fear. If you were bitten by a poisonous snake, you would want to remove all the poison, not just some of it. The smart thing to do is to repeat this exercise with any fear that you have.

Holding onto fear is creating trouble for yourself. But when you bring up all your fear and let it all go, you can live in happiness, harmony, and abundance.

> *My panic attacks are gone. I only feel peace now. Thank you for this wonderful technique!*
>
> — TW, Wisconsin

> *I had severe anxiety getting on the freeway. It was preventing me from having a life because I couldn't go anywhere. I used this method and dumped that phobia. It was so simple. I couldn't believe how easy it was. I now look at life in such a way that it becomes magical.*
>
> — LB, California

ANGER

Holding onto anger is very detrimental to your health, your relationships, your money-making ability, and your overall happiness. Remaining in anger about something is like "drinking poison and waiting for the other guy to die." You also suffer when you hold onto anger by trying to "stuff" or suppress it.

But there is a way for you to rid yourself of all your anger without suppressing or expressing it. Are you ready to experience it?

Ok, so think of something that you have anger about.

Now, on a scale from 1 to 10, with 10 being the most angry and 1 being the least angry, where are you right now with regard to the anger? I can show you a way to get rid of that anger if you are willing

102

to do something different. Are you willing to do something different?

Can you see that you have been saying "No" to the anger? You don't like the anger, do you? You have been saying "No" to it, right? But when you say "No" to it, you're actually collecting it. So now can you say "Yes" to the anger so that you can get rid of it? Can you say "Yes" to the anger some more? And more? And even more? And can you say "Yes" to it again? And "Yes" again? And can you say "Yes" to the anger even more? And more? And even more?

Now take a check on the scale from 1-10, where are you now with regard to the anger? Notice that saying "Yes" to it actually lowers your amount of anger. Now that your anger is lower on the scale, you have an indication that you are headed in the right direction. Saying "Yes" to the anger allows you to get rid of it, while saying "No" to it was only collecting the anger.

So now instead of pushing down on it, can you just invite it up? Can you say "Yes" to the remaining anger and just let it come up and out?

Continue repeating this exercise on the anger until you are at zero on the scale with regard to the anger. If you were bitten by a poisonous snake, you would want to remove all the poison, not just some of it. When you let go of all the anger you move into love, harmony, and abundance in all areas of your life.

I have been able to control my frustration and anger about things going on in my life and with people in my life. I have gained the ability to control pain, tiredness and hunger.

— PH, Texas (age 14)

PAIN

I learned to start loving pain instead of disapproving of it and to love myself more and more and the pain is gone.

—AW, United Kingdom

Many people resist pain or try to suppress or get away from it. But resisting, suppressing, or trying to escape the pain never actually reduces or removes it. Why not? The reason is simple. Pain is just a signal from your body, like a doorbell ringing, saying "please fix me." So if you never answer the door, the pain never goes away. The way out of pain is to go toward it. Answer the "doorbell" and allow your body to resolve whatever was going on that caused the pain signal.

Try this exercise and you'll see what I mean. Are you ready?

So get in touch with the pain you are feeling.

Now, on a scale from 1 to 10, with 10 being the most painful and 1 being the least painful, where are you right now with regard to the pain?

I can show you a way to get rid of the pain if you are willing to do something different.

Are you willing to do something different?

Can you see that you have been saying "No" to the pain? You don't like the pain, do you? You have been saying "No" to it, right? But when you say "No" to it, you're not "answering the doorbell" and you are actually collecting the pain.

So now can you say "Yes" to the pain so that you can get rid of it? Can you say "Yes" to the pain some more? And more? And even more? And can you say "Yes" to it again? And "Yes" again? And can you say "Yes" to the pain even more? And more? And even more?

Now take a check. On the scale from 1-10, where are you now with regard to the pain? Notice that saying "Yes" to it actually lowers your amount of pain. Now that your pain is lower on the scale, you have an indication that you are headed in the right direction. Saying "Yes" to the pain allows you to get rid of it, while saying "No" to it was only collecting the pain.

So now instead of pushing down on it, can you just invite it up? Can you say "Yes" to the remaining pain and just let it come up and out?

Continue repeating this exercise on the pain until you are at zero on the scale with regard to the pain. If you were bitten by a poisonous snake, you would want to remove all the poison not just some of it. By "answering the doorbell" and letting the pain go, you allow your body to move into complete harmony and health.

> *I'm a disabled Viet Nam Veteran. For the last 25 years, I have been beating myself up. I never felt good. In just two days with this technique, I'm feeling much better. This has changed my life.*
>
> — PL, California

> *I hurt my ankle. I experienced tremendous pain. I started using this technique and the pain went away quickly and without medication. I never had to see a doctor about it.*
>
> — PD, New York

> *I had painful colitis flare up and was able to clear the pain using this method.*
>
> — GMS, California

Now let's move on to another extremely valuable exercise that will change your life if you practice it.

Quickly Move From Negative to Positive

> *I realized approval and loving oneself is all healing.*
>
> — RD, New Jersey

In the past, when you've had a situation you haven't been able to resolve, a question you haven't been able to answer, or problem you haven't been able to find a solution to, you follow a pattern you may not even be aware of up to now.

The pattern leaves you feeling more and more frustrated, more and more confused and further away from getting your answer or solving your problem. You've had things you've been going around and around with for years, trying to get an answer or trying to solve, and you still don't have your answer or solution. In this book, you've seen that loving yourself is the answer to all of your questions and leads to solving any problem.

Now, in order to have something different, you must be willing to do something different. You see that, don't you? If you always do what you've always done, you always have what you've always gotten, right?

In the following exercises, covering several situations people commonly face, I'm going to show you how to get off that merry-go-round you've been on and actually be able to get answers and find solutions.

You have to be willing to do something different. What you've done up to now in your life hasn't worked, has it? Are you willing to do something different so you can have a different result than you've been getting?

* * *

Remember, to get the most out of these exercises it is necessary to "play along." Focus your attention and answer back as I ask you the questions, rather than merely reading through this section. These are experiential (not intellectual) exercises. So, to experience, you must participate. Let's get started.

MONEY, FINANCES

Let's begin with finances, money, credit card debt. Do you have a money issue that you haven't been able to resolve in your life?

Ask your mind if it knows how to get you out of this money problem.

It doesn't know does it? So asking something that doesn't know is like looking in an empty file cabinet for an answer that's not there and you keep looking. Can you see how silly that is? Now your friend your mind has been telling you to beat yourself up for not getting your answer, hasn't it? Has beating yourself up helped you resolve your money situation? It hasn't helped at all at all, has it?

And who's doing it, who's beating up on yourself? You are, of course.

All right, if you're doing it and it doesn't get your answer or resolve the situation, you have a decision to make: You're going to be positive and love yourself, or your going to continue to be negative and beat yourself up. What do you decide?

I'm assuming you decided to be positive and love yourself. Good. That's smart. So, can you let go of disapproving of yourself? And can you let go of disapproving of yourself some more?

And can you let go of disapproving of yourself some more, and more, and more. Now, can you give yourself some approval? Can you give yourself some more approval? And give yourself some more approval? And more? And even more?

Now check, does it feel more possible or less possible to resolve your money situation than it did just a couple of minutes ago? More possible, right?

Ok, good. That lets you know you're headed in the right direction. The law of the universe is "positive attracts positive, and negative attracts negative."

So keep going and you'll see the results, keeping letting go of asking your mind, keep letting go of disapproving and send approval. It works if you do it. Prove it to yourself.

I learned to smother myself with love...my pain and fear about money disappeared.

— LM, California

Here is what I received for the first three months of using the method of loving myself. Within one week my debt of R8000 was cancelled. I got a new office in Kempton Park and saved rental money in the process. I paid up my clothing debts of R3200 and credit card debt of R8500. I employed a helper at my business, as it was now very busy. My income increased from about R1000 to R73000 per month. I bought myself a Mercedes Benz. I saved R3500 from the loss Telekom shares. In fact, I gained when others lost. This works. I am always happy all the time. Even my dog stops barking, just by giving it approval. If this method can work for me in Africa it can surely work for anyone. Thank you!

— SM, Tembisa, South Africa

Now let's say your money problem is credit card debt. It could be several other things such as your job or your income. Whatever it is, you see it as a negative situation, right? You don't like it. You're disapproving of it. Do you see what you're doing? You have a negative situation, and you're pouring more negative on the situation when you're disapproving of it. How is that ever going to do anything but make the negative situation more negative?

So, I can show you how to get rid of that negativity and get started turning your finances around but you're going to have to be willing to do something different than you've been doing. Are you willing to do that?

You've been asking your mind if it knows how to get you out of the credit card debt, haven't you? But it doesn't know, does it?

So asking something that doesn't know is like looking in an empty file cabinet for an answer that's not there, and you keep looking.

Can you see how silly that is? Now your friend your mind has been telling you to disapprove of your credit card debt, hasn't it?

How has disapproving of your credit card debt helped you? It hasn't helped at all at all, has it? And, who is doing it? You are.

All right, if you're doing it and it doesn't resolve the situation, now you have a decision to make: Be positive and love your credit card debt, or continue being negative and disapproving of it. What do you decide?

You decided to be positive and love your credit card debt, didn't you? Some people new to this idea of being loving instead of being hating have trouble with giving approval to something they see as negative like credit card debt. Ask yourself a question. Has what you've been doing worked? Has pouring negative energy out solved your credit card debt? Positive energy, love, approval is transforming, it transforms negative into positive. That's why it's a smart idea to let go of the negative, disapproval and send positive, approval to any situation.

Back to the credit card debt. So, can you let go of disapproving of the credit card debt? Can you let go of disapproving of it some more, and some more? Good.

Now, can you give some approval to the credit card debt? Can you give it some more approval? And, give it some approval and more and more.

Now check. Does it feel more possible or less possible to resolve your money situation than it did just a couple of minutes ago? More possible, right? Ok, good. That lets you know you're headed in the right direction. The law of the universe is "positive attracts positive, and negative attracts negative."

> *Last year, I was totally broke. I couldn't make a living. I used this Technique and I am now making $75,000 and going up, each month.*
>
> — LS, California

So keep going and you'll see the results, keep letting go of asking your mind, keep letting go of disapproving and send approval. Keep it up and you will see that it works.

Whatever your money problem is, whatever your job problem is, whatever your income problem is, you can change it for the better in no time at all, if you practice this exercise.

> *Once I learned to love myself, I increased my income from an unemployment check to $30,000 a month within a year and a half. If I can do it, anybody can.*
>
> — JW, Minnesota

If you've been working along with the words, rather than merely reading them, you've noticed you've gotten a bit more positive. If you've been reading the words rather than working along with the words, you may be resisting the repetition of what is being said. You may be thinking, he isn't doing anything but repeating the same thing over and over. Your mind might be telling you to get agitated a little bit.

Lester Levenson said, "If there's anything I do, it's repeat the same thing over and over and over and over again." Lester did it because he knew that repetition is a good way to learn and if you have something that works, do it over and over and over and over again.

The way I am showing you here, letting go of asking your mind, letting go of disapproving and sending approval is a technique that we know works. It works if you do it. It works if you repeat it. That's the reason for the repetition.

Now, on to the subject of relationships.

RELATIONSHIPS

> *I am able to have easier and better relationships with others and I feel more love for people. I am feeling lighter and freer and have much more joy in my everyday living.*
>
> — LH, Missouri

How about relationships? How are your relationships working for you? Have you been trying to figure out how to resolve a relationship situation? Have you been going around and around in your head trying to figure out what you should do or how you should do it?

You've been asking your mind for an answer. It doesn't have an answer for you does it? Well, let's check right now. Ask your mind if it knows how to get you out of this relationship problem. Go ahead, ask it.

It doesn't know, does it? So asking something that doesn't know is like looking in an empty file cabinet for an answer and you keep looking. Can you see how silly that is?

Now your friend your mind has been telling you to beat yourself up for not being able to resolve this relationship situation, hasn't it? Has beating yourself up helped you resolve your relationship situation? It hasn't helped at all at all, has it? And who's doing it, who is beating up on yourself? You are.

All right, if you're doing it and it doesn't get your answer or resolve the situation, you have a decision to make: You are going to be positive and love yourself, or you're going to be negative and beat yourself up. What do you decide? I'm assuming you decided to be positive and love yourself. Good. That's smart.

So, can you let go of disapproving of yourself? And can you let go of disapproving of yourself some more? And can you let go of disapproving of yourself some more and more, and more?

Now, since you decided to be positive and love yourself, can you give yourself some approval right now? Can you give yourself some more approval? Can you give yourself some more approval, just because? And more? And can you give yourself some more approval? And more? And even more?

Now check, does it feel more possible or less possible to resolve your relationship situation than it did just a couple of minutes ago? More possible, right?

Ok, good. That lets you know you're headed in the right direction now and the law of the universe is "positive attracts positive, and negative attracts negative." So, keep going and you'll see the results, keep letting go of asking your mind, keep letting go of disapproving and send approval.

> *Using this technique, I gained a new trust level with my wife and new understanding in our excellent relationship that took it to a new level. Our abundance increased as we moved into action and we had a $75,000 windfall.*
>
> — JG, Arizona

> *I have been feeling more love and approval for myself and everyone else than ever before. When I catch myself in disapproval, I can let go of it immediately. I even had dinner with my mother, who knows the right buttons to push more than anyone else, and felt like I was floating on a cloud!*
>
> — KW, California

Now how about the other person in the relationship? Ask your mind if it knows how to get the other person to work with you to solve this relationship problem. Go ahead and ask it. It doesn't know, does it? So asking something that doesn't know is like looking in an empty file cabinet for an answer and you keep looking. Can you see how silly that is?

Now your friend your mind has been telling you to disapprove of the person hasn't it? Has disapproving of them helped resolve your relationship situation? It hasn't helped at all at all, has it? And who's doing it? Who's disapproving of them? You are.

All right, if you're doing it and it doesn't get your answer or resolve the situation, you have a decision to make: You can be positive and love the other person, or you can be negative and keep disapproving of them. What do you decide?

I'm assuming you decided to be positive and love them. Good. Very smart.

So, can you let go of disapproving of that person? And can you let go of disapproving of them some more? And can you let go of disapproving of the other person some more? And more, and more?

Now, can you give the person some approval? Can you give them some more approval? And can you give them some more approval? And more? And more?

Now check, does it feel more possible or less possible to resolve the relationship situation than it did just a couple of minutes ago? More possible, right? Ok, good. That lets you know you're headed in the right direction. The law of the universe is "positive attracts positive, and negative attracts negative."

> *About 6 months ago I started using what I call "projecting love" to people. I use it all the time now. For example, we get together a lot for family activities. At these gatherings I silently say to each person (around 40 of them) "I love you" over and over silently. One of my sons-in-law who has been a little cool to me over the years, is now very friendly! Also, my brother-in-law who has purposely bugged me for the last 53 years is now very friendly and never says anything negative about me! In fact, he even complemented my clothes (unheard of). On top of that, when they got back to Orlando, FL, they even sent me an email to tell me how great I looked at Thanksgiving!! Believe me, my clothes were no different than I ever wear. Additionally, I use "I love you" silently for one fellow who always sees the world as black and negative (he calls it "being realistic"). Now he seeks me out for hugs where before, even when I wanted to give him a hug, he was reluctant because he felt unworthy.*
>
> — Ralph Miller, Texas

So, keep going and you'll see the results, keep letting go of asking your mind, keep letting go of disapproving and send approval.

There is absolutely no reason not to have wonderful, warm, loving relationships with everyone you know.

RELATIONSHIP EXERCISE

You found out earlier in the book that to be loving, you first let go of the non-love feelings called disapproval. Disapproval is not-liking this or that, not-liking this person or that person. Not-liking this or that thing. Not-liking this or that situation. Any "not-liking" is disapproval. Disapproval is negative.

When you are into not-liking people and things you are collecting negativity. You are storing up non-love feelings and are in the direction of unhappiness, non-abundance, sickness and troubled relationships with people in your world.

Letting go of the "not-liking" feelings, called disapproval, is a must. You can practice letting go of disapproval and sending approval. You decide, this disapproval does not help me. I'm doing it. Since I'm doing it and it doesn't help me I need to make a decision. The decision is be positive and loving or be negative and non-loving. I'm sure you decided to be positive. You get positive by letting go of the negative.

> *Using this method I now have the ability to love uncon-ditionally the person who in the past I always blamed for everything "wrong" in my life (my mom).*
>
> — CP, New York

Here is the exercise:

Make a list of all the people or things in your life that you do not like. Write them all down.

Now, start going through each person or thing on your list. For each person or thing on your list, do the following. Ask your mind if it knows how to resolve the relationship or fix the thing you are disapproving of. Ask your mind.

114

Your mind doesn't know, does it? It's like looking in an empty file cabinet for an answer that's not there and you keep looking. Can you see how silly that is?

Now your friend your mind has told you to beat yourself up about not being able to resolve the relationship or patch-up the thing, hasn't it? (It's also telling you to disapprove of the person or thing, isn't it?). Does the disapproval help you? You know the disapproval does not help you. And who is doing it? You're doing it.

Since you're doing it and it doesn't help, you need to make a decision. I'm going to be positive and love myself (and them) or I'm going to be negative and disapprove of myself (or them).

What did you decide? I'm sure you decided to be positive. You get positive by letting go of the negative.

So, can you let go of disapproving of yourself? And more? And more? (Let go of disapproving until there is no more disapproval.)

Now, since you decided to be positive and love yourself, can you give yourself some approval? And more? And more approval?

Now can you let go of disapproving of the person or thing or situation? And keep letting go of the disapproval until you don't notice any more disapproval.

Then, can you give that person (or thing or situation) some approval? And more approval? And more? And more?

> *I dramatically improved relationships with family members by sending them love. As an offshoot my health improved, my blood pressure is normal. Now, I'm looking forward to making new friends.*
>
> — PS, Arizona

Do this exercise for each person or thing on your list that you don't like. Do it thoroughly for each person, or thing, or situation past and present.

How do you know you have been thorough? You know you have been thorough when you have only feelings of love and trust for the person, thing or situation. Then move on to the next one on your list.

Right now your mind may be telling you a lot of things about doing this exercise: "It's too daunting, there are too many on that list, it will take forever," and on and on. That's what your mind could be saying. Guess what? That's the reason to do it. Do it and have great positive results.

All the not liking, disapproval, is negative energy in you. Negative energy blocks the flow of positive, loving energy. Negative energy blocks you from abundance, happiness, success and all good things in life.

> *I am able to love and accept myself and my prospects and clients, even when I am being brutally "rejected." The result is that everything is becoming increasingly easy.*
>
> — CP, New York

Do this exercise. It may take a while to get through your list. However, rewards are waiting for you as you do this exercise. You are getting more and more loving and positive with each one on your list that you complete. More love and more goodness begins flowing your way. And, this exercise is making you more and more aware of what you've been doing all your life. More important, it is waking you up to what you are doing everyday. Seeing that, you begin practicing letting go of disapproval, letting go of not liking people and things, before it gets past your nose. And then you have only love in your life and love and all things positive flow to you.

GREAT HEALTH

You've been trying to figure out what to do about your body, your health, haven't you? You're not alone. It's a habit human beings picked up somewhere along the line. You like to think about how you can have better health. Even people in great health think about it. How can I have even better health? How's my body doing? Is everything OK? Is everything working like it should?

Those with less than good health spend even more time at it. Those with health problems spend a lot of time thinking about their body and wondering how they can restore it to good health. They wonder how they got this health problem. They wonder what to do about it.

The other habit humans picked up along the way is disapproving. Not liking is the same as disapproval. So, you have an ache or pain. You have a cold or flu. You have a diagnosis. Maybe you have a very serious, life-threatening condition or disease. The habit you have, that all humans have (unless they have become acquainted with this information and broken the habit) is to disapprove of their body, the body problem, the health problem. You don't like it. You disapprove of it. As you've learned, disapproval is negative energy.

The thing you're disapproving of, the body condition or pain, is a pocket of negative energy. Do you see that? And what are you doing? You're pouring more negative energy on it when you don't like it, when you disapprove of it. You are pouring negative energy on the negative energy. How does that help the body problem? How does that resolve the pain? It doesn't. It adds to it. It makes it worse.

Someone could be asking, "Well, what am I supposed to do? Love it? " I'll let you answer that one for yourself. Of course, you're welcome to keep up the disapproval if you think it helps you. You can do that. But I think you agree, negativity has never done anything for you. You know it's never gotten you anywhere. Again, don't believe a word I'm saying. Prove it to yourself. If loving it and giving approval doesn't work, after you have given it a fair effort, then you can always go back to beating yourself up.

So, you see that you have been pouring negative energy on your body and your body condition. I can show you how to resolve your health problem but you're going to have to be willing to do something different than you've been doing. You already agreed that hasn't worked for you. Are you willing to do something different in order to have a different result? I assume you said, yes.

Ok. Ask your mind if it knows how to have a healthy body. Go ahead, ask it. It doesn't know does it? So asking something that doesn't know is like looking in an empty file cabinet for an answer and you keep looking. Can you see how silly that is?

Now your friend your mind has been telling you to beat yourself up for not being able to resolve this health situation, hasn't it? Has beating yourself up helped you resolve your health situation? It hasn't helped at all, has it? And, who's doing it? Who's beating up on yourself? You are, of course.

All right, if you're doing it and it doesn't get your answer or resolve the situation, you have a decision to make: You are going to be positive and love yourself, or you're going to be negative and beat yourself up. What do you decide? I'm assuming you decided to be positive and love yourself. Good. That's smart.

So, can you let go of disapproving of yourself? And can you let go of disapproving of yourself some more? And, can you let go of disapproving of yourself some more? And more? And more? Now, can you give yourself some approval? Can you give yourself some more approval? And, can you give yourself some more approval? And more? And more?

Now check, does it feel more possible or less possible to have a healthy body than it did just a couple of minutes ago? More possible, right? Ok, good.

My blood pressure was high. My cholesterol was high. I was having frequent anxiety. I was taking blood pressure medication, cholesterol medication, and anti-anxiety medication. Using this technique, it has all turned around: No more medication of any kind; Deep, restful sleep; relaxed, confident attitude; More patience toward my son, my wife

and myself; Relief of neck, shoulder and back pain; And, a
relaxed approach to relationships and situations.

— CM, Michigan

That lets you know you're headed in the right direction. The law of the universe is "positive attracts positive, and negative attracts negative." So, keep going and you'll see the results, keep letting go of asking your mind, keep letting go of disapproving and send approval. There is absolutely no reason not to have a healthy body all the time.

A DIAGNOSIS

I saw major improvement in my diagnosis, which included
symptoms of bronchitis and sinusitis. For the first time I was
able to look into the mirror and say, I love you and I approve
of you.

— LK, Texas

Some people have a diagnosis.

Ask your mind if it knows what to do about the diagnosis. Go ahead, ask it. It doesn't know does it? So asking something that doesn't know is like looking in an empty file cabinet for an answer and you keep looking. Can you see how silly that is? Now your friend your mind has been telling you to disapprove of the diagnosis, hasn't it? Has disapproving of it helped you resolve the diagnosis? It hasn't helped at all at all, has it? And who's doing it, who's disapproving of the diagnosis? You are, of course.

All right, if you're doing it and it doesn't get your answer or resolve the situation, you have a decision to make: You are going to be positive and love the diagnosis, or you're going to be negative and disapprove of the diagnosis. What do you decide? I'm assuming you decided to be positive and love the diagnosis. Good. That's smart.

So, can you let go of disapproving of the diagnosis? And can you let go of disapproving of the diagnosis some more? And can you let go of disapproving of the diagnosis some more, and more, and even more?

Now, can you give the diagnosis some approval? Can you give the diagnosis some more approval? And give the diagnosis some more approval, and more, and more.

Now check, does it feel more possible or less possible to resolve the diagnosis than it did just a couple of minutes ago? More possible, right? Ok, good. That lets you know you're headed in the right direction. The law of the universe is "positive attracts positive, and negative attracts negative." So, keep going and you'll see the results, keep letting go of asking your mind, keep letting go of disapproving and give approval. There is absolutely no reason not to have vibrant health.

> *I was told by my surgeons and two other doctors that I had only three months to live. They said, I had arteriosclerosis, 80% blockage of my heart. I had black and blue skin on both my legs, dizziness, forgetfulness, high blood pressure, and I was on five medications daily. I started using the technique and immediately my health changed for the better. It has been one year and all my illnesses are gone. Not only that I received $40,000 I got out of the blue, the most money I've ever had in my life. My daughter used the technique to rid herself of anger and rage.*
>
> — JR, Texas

> *All symptoms of Parkinson's have disappeared and my increased strength and outlook have me re-energized. The doctors can't believe this happened.*
>
> — ST, Ohio

PAIN

My shoulders hurt but I gave them approval and now the pain is gone. I walked across a bridge in the woods and knew that bridge represented me being able to be in love with myself permanently now.

— OL, New York

This method works well to resolve pain.

Ask your mind if it knows how to get rid of pain. Go ahead, ask it.

It doesn't know does it? So asking something that doesn't know is like looking in an empty file cabinet for an answer and you keep looking. Can you see how silly that is?

I had several physical ailments including migraine head-aches, diverticulitis, gout and severe hypoglycemia. The week after I began using this method, I was scheduled for surgery. Within a few days, the surgical condition disap-peared and never re-appeared. My other physical problems cleared up. I believe these good effects are due to the stress reduction brought about by using this method.

— David Hawkins, M.D., Manhasset, New York

Now your friend your mind has been telling you to disapprove of the pain, hasn't it? Has disapproving of it helped you resolve the pain? It hasn't helped at all at all, has it? And who's doing it, who's disapproving of the pain? You are, of course.

All right, if you're doing it and it doesn't get your answer or resolve the situation, you have a decision to make: You are going to be posi-tive and love the pain, or you're going to be negative and disapprove of the pain. What do you decide? I'm assuming you decided to be positive and love the pain. Good. That's smart.

So, can you let go of disapproving of the pain? And can you let go of disapproving of the pain some more? And can you let go of disapproving of the pain some more and more, and more?

"I had aches in my right arm for approximately 20 years. I let go of disapproving of the pain and gave it approval and released the pain. I am sleeping better. I allow myself to be happier and to get closer to people and talk to them."

— ES, California

Now, can you give the pain some approval? Can you give the pain some more approval? And can you give the pain some more approval? And more? And more?

Now check, does it feel more possible or less possible to resolve the pain than it did just a couple of minutes ago? More possible, right? Ok, good. That lets you know you're headed in the right direction. The law of the universe is "positive attracts positive, and negative attracts negative."

I am able to rid my body of pain that arises within a short period of time. It's a matter of letting go of disapproval of the pain and giving it approval so it can leave.

— David Durand, M.D., New York

So, keep going and you'll see the results, keep letting go of asking your mind, keep letting go of disapproving and send approval. There is absolutely no reason not to have a pain free body.

This method works, if you do it. Isn't it worth a try? Lester let go of his negative, non-love feelings, he cured his body and never saw a doctor again in 40 years. Lester showed you the way. It's up to you to do it. It works if you do it.

The doctor couldn't believe it.

While making popcorn the old-fashioned way, I ended up burning my hand/thumb from the steam.

The pain was terrible. I've had two kids with no drugs and no pain killers...this burn hurt 1000 times worse. Icing it simply kept me from slitting my wrists. For six hours I kept ice on it directly and needed to get to sleep.

I would lay down and the pain got worse. After several attempts of trying to sleep, I got dressed and headed down to the 24 hour drug store to get some burn cream and sleeping pills. The pain medication barely touched the pain, but I felt like I could maybe sleep. I got into bed and the throbbing pain increased. Then, I finally remembered: I sent the pain love and approval for ten minutes and. . . gee, I must have dozed off.

I woke up the next morning with absolutely no awareness or sensation that something was wrong. Then I remembered. Whoa, what happened to all that excruciating pain six hours ago? There was NONE. Not even a little bit. There was no redness, no swelling, no huge blister you might expect. COOL!!!!! I went through the day PAIN FREE. I went to sleep that night pain free. I woke up the next morning, pain free.

Around noon, a blister began to form. It didn't hurt, but it got bigger and bigger. I kind of looked at it like it was pretty cool and gave it approval and watched, still no pain. By the next afternoon, the blister was pushing maximum density and I caved in to everybody badgering me that I should see a doctor. (I went to basically shut my husband up.)

When I told the doctor what happened and went through the whole sequence of events, she kept asking:

'When did the blister show up? What ELSE did you do? (as in, treatment) It doesn't hurt, AT ALL? Are you sure you didn't put anything else on it? She couldn't believe it all happened because I gave it love and approval. I attribute the whole thing to remembering to love it.'

— LR, Pittsburgh

123

GET ALL THE GOODNESS

As Lester said, you are spiraling upward.

A quick, easy and very pleasant way to turn yourself positive is to let go of disapproval and give approval, to let go of disapproving of yourself and give yourself approval. If you are feeling a little off, or maybe a lot off, there is no better way to turn it around than by letting go of disapproving of yourself and giving yourself approval.

Let go of disapproving of yourself and give yourself approval throughout your day. It will change your life.

All the happiness in the universe is in you, so you get more of the happiness as you let go of the unhappiness.

When you feel inclined to stop during the exercise of giving yourself approval, it is just your signal that there is some subconscious disapproval there. And trying to give yourself approval while subconsciously disapproving of yourself is like trying to drive your car with the emergency brake on (only you don't know it's on). So it is very simple to handle. Just let go of the disapproval then you can go back to giving yourself approval.

Your mind brings up a lot of disapproval, which is a great benefit. That disapproval has been hiding out in your subconscious mind. You didn't know it was there. Now it's up into your awareness and you let it go, never to be bothered by that piece of negativity again.

So, the assignment is to give yourself approval for as long and as often as you can. If it's 5 seconds or 5 hours or anywhere in between, it is good because it's in the direction of positive. Positive attracts positive. So when you are positive, you find you have more and more positive in your life. You cannot do anything better for yourself, for your family, for the world.

Prove it to yourself.

"The fastest and surest way to health and prosperity is Love."

— Lester Levenson

CHAPTER FIFTEEN

INSIGHTS ON LOVE

One day, before I learned releasing, I got my fingers pinched in my stroller. I got very upset and very scared. An ambulance came and wrapped my fingers up for me. But, I stayed upset and scared that it would happen again. It took a long time for my fingers to get better (mom says about two weeks). Then, once I started releasing and my whole family was releasing, one day my fingers got closed in the sliding door of the van. My mom picked me up and asked me if I could love my fingers. I started loving my fingers instead of getting upset and scared. My brother was calm instead of being upset because he was loving my fingers and loving what happened too. I kept sitting and loving my fingers, more and more and more. Only a little while later that same day, my fingers were great.

— Vivian, Age 5 (as told to her mother)

How to find Love.

"I was looking for love in all the wrong places

Looking for love in too many faces

Searching your eyes, looking for traces Of what.. I'm dreaming of...

Hopin' to find a friend and a lover

God bless the day I discover

Another heart, lookin' for love"

You probably recognize the words from the Waylon Jennings song.

That is how many people in this world spend their entire lives, looking for love in too many faces.

They're looking for love exactly where it is not, out there. Maybe when they were in that crib with those doting adults hovering over them, maybe that's when they first decided love is out there. Maybe that was when they decided to find love, to get love, to be loved, you have to get it out there. You have to get it from someone. They have to give it to you. If you can't get someone to love you, you live in misery and constant wanting. You're looking for love in all the wrong places.

Lester Levenson made a discovery. He found that when he was looking for love, when he wanted love from others, he was sick, and miserable and suffering. When he wanted to be loved he was living in negativity.

Lester found that the times in his life when he was loving, he was positive, happy, healthy and wealthy.

Lester saw that when he wanted to be loved, he wanted something from someone. He wanted them to love him so you he could feel good. Lester saw that's the opposite of love. He realized it's non-loving to want someone to love us.

He found out that love is an attitude of givingness. It is an attitude of givingness to another, with no thought of receiving anything in return. Love is wanting the other person to have what they want even though you can't to give it to them.

Lester made this discovery and set out to rid himself of all of his non-loving feelings. He found what was left was the all loving, infinite being he always was. He healed his body. His healed his entire life. Lester showed us the way. To find love, look inside and there it is. Love is right inside of you, covered up by non-love feelings.

We just do not love ourselves enough. I am letting go of disapproving of myself and giving myself approval everyday. That information is priceless. I finally opened my eyes and saw that I cannot get approval from others which I was doing because, they do not have it themselves. The only answer is giving myself approval and loving myself, and it is inside ME.

— Carmen, Hawaii

You search around in all those eyes and then one day you spot the perfect someone. You "fall in love" with them. It's someone just like you. This someone wants love from you, and you want love from them. That's what we call a relationship. You soon discover this other person doesn't have love to give you. They want you to give them love. So, two people, both wanting love from the other one and each not having it to give.

Is it any wonder we have such a high rate of divorce, so many family problems, so much anger and frustration? We're looking for love in all the wrong places.

You do not have to go anywhere to find all the love in the universe. It's right inside of you right now where it's always been. Let go of the non-love feelings and find out. You're opening up to the natural all loving being that you are, always have been, always will be.

It's not easy for you to see. Because, for a long time, you've had a habit of chasing love where it isn't. For a long time, you've had a habit of looking for love out there. Realize, there is nothing to do. There is nowhere to go. All the love in the universe is right here, right where you are. You are that right now.

I now know that I have all the love I could possibly want. I now know, experientially, that I never have to "look for love" (anywhere) again! Oh the joy and free feeling that brings; it is indescribable!

— PM, California

I have been practicing giving love and approval. I went to a woman's home to give her an estimate for my service. As I was giving my estimate, I kept feeling so much love for the woman and for myself. We finished up and she said she would be getting other estimates. The next morning, the woman called me and said, "We have decided to go with you. There's something about you. And, I feel really good about you."

That same day, five people called for estimates (at a typically, very slow time). I scheduled three estimates that week and closed all three. All three of the people said some version of, "I feel confident with you. I feel good about going with you." I'm telling you. This is magic!

— KW, California

Decide To Have a Wonderful Loving Day.

I drive about 70 miles round trip to commute to my office in San Francisco, in sometimes snail-like traffic over the Bay Bridge. I decided to send approval to it all and love the ride. In fact, I've written a "Love Song to Commuting" that I sing on my way to and from San Francisco every day. I now arrive quite refreshed and peaceful, and I have happy trips, no matter who is on the road or what is happening "out there."

— Deborah, California

You determine your life, your happiness and your love. You decide. Whatever you hold in your mind all the time is what you get.

Have an intention for everything you do. An intention is a mini-goal. Without intention, you are thrown around by the waves of the ocean of life. You can land almost anywhere, including landing on the rocks. Having an intention for everything you do is deciding in advance

130

where you are going and where you will land. With intention you set your sails, and you sail where you intended.

Have an intention for everything you do. Start your day with intentions. Keep an eye on them to be sure you stay on course throughout your day.

Make it your intention, to be loving in spite of whatever happens. Decide to have your life run by love. Fuel your day with love, the most powerful force in the universe. When you are loving, you experience love.

Remember that love and being loving, is living in the same energy as being positive, being happy, being successful and being abundant.

The intention to be loving is a decision to live in the energy of love, the highest energy. I decide. I am loving all day long no matter what anyone is doing or saying. No matter what the news is saying, no matter what my spouse says, no matter what my children say, no matter what my boss says, no matter my bank account, no matter a body ache or pain, I am loving.

Have the intention to be loving, whatever comes your way. That is holding in mind love. What you hold in mind is what you experience all the time. Your intention to be loving and holding in mind love guarantees you positive energy. It guarantees you success. It guarantees you abundance. It guarantees you vibrant health. It guarantees you peaceful, stress-free living. It's guaranteed because that's what you're holding in mind.

> *I'm sleeping better than I have for years. I quit taking drugs for arthritis and feel much better without it. Everything is improving in my life.*
>
> — BL, Ohio

Practice it. Prove it to yourself.

Make it your intention. Be loving. Watch what happens.

Yours is the world and all that's in it.

Have the intention to be loving and find out.

You Have All the Riches.

Keep it Simple Sweetheart.

Lester Levenson told us why we're unhappy. He showed us what to do about it. He said, "Keep it Simple Sweetheart." However, your mind does not want to keep it simple. Your mind wants to complicate it. Your mind says the reason you're unhappy is complicated. Lester said, "Whatever you see as complicated, is not complicated. You mind is complicated."

The reason you're unhappy is very simple. You're unhappy due to non-love feelings. Non-love feelings make you unhappy and keep you unhappy. The solution is simple. Let go of the non-love feelings. Get love, get happiness, by letting go of what is making you unhappy, the non-love, disapproval feelings.

Your mind wants to make your life more complicated. You have the answer why you're unhappy, but you're driven by your mind to keep on searching. Your mind tells you there must be something else. "There must be something I'm missing. I have to read that new book. I have to check into that new organization I heard about." You can't satisfy your mind. That's why your mind keeps making noise even after you have the answer to every question you ever asked. You've been shown the answer, but your mind wants you to think it's something else.

In the story *Acres of Diamonds*, by Russell Conwell, the farmer, Hafid, is desperate for wealth but he sees none on his meager farm. He sells his farm and travels all over the world seeking his fortune. He finds nothing but despair and anguish. Meanwhile the man who bought Hafid's old farm found one of the richest diamond mines ever discovered on that very same land. Hafid had been sitting on the fabulous riches of his dreams all along, thinking they were somewhere else.

Right now, you are sitting on your riches. You are searching for love everywhere it isn't, just like Hafid. You have all the love in the universe right where you are. You don't have to go anywhere. All you have to do is uncover your wealth by letting go of the non-love feelings.

All there is to it, is to do it.

> *I know I can love everything and anything all the time. I can love my mind. I can love my feelings. I can love my body. Can anything be more powerful than that?*
>
> — ES, New York

Happiness is Loving.

Think of someone you don't like. Maybe it's someone who bothers you. Can you love them?

No one said you have to love what they do or what they say. However, you can love the infinite, eternal being that they are.

"Why do I have to love them?" Do you find yourself asking that?

Let's begin by saying it's smart to love everyone and everything. It's smart because being loving is being positive, being positive is being abundant, and being abundant is being happy.

"All right, I can be positive. However, that particular politician or that criminal, do I have to love them?" It's a decision. Be positive and loving or be negative and non-loving. You might think you're sending negative energy out there when you don't like someone. However, the negative energy is in you when your words or your thinking are non-loving.

When you express non-loving feelings toward anyone or anything, your mind somehow thinks you're "getting" them, you're "getting them real good" and they deserve it. Notice what's really going on. You're "getting" someone all right. You're getting you. You're getting yourself down when you're putting out negative energy.

It's a moment-to-moment decision. You can be positive and loving or you can be negative and non-loving.

Aren't we humans funny? We really think negativity somehow brings something positive to us. How can that possibly be true? How does negative bring about something that is positive? Negative brings about more negativity. Positive brings about love, it brings about success, it brings about happiness, and it brings about abundance.

Non-loving feelings are a bad habit we picked-up along the way. For some silly reason we think it does something for us. What it does is make us sick, miserable, and lacking in abundance.

You want to have it both ways: Love the people and things you decide to love and hate the people and things you decide to hate. Could it be, that's why sometimes you feel joyful and a lot of the time you feel miserable? Getting into that love/hate mind-game, it's easy to forget whose side you're on a lot of the time. The line gets blurred and soon the number of people you love is far fewer than the number of people you hate. Look closely. Notice you're on the side of negativity anytime you're anything but all loving, all positive.

What is the answer?

Bail out the barrel. When you bail out the non-loving feelings, it's like bailing water out of a barrel one scoop at a time. As you bail, you make room for the positive to flow in. For every scoop you bail, love flows in and transforms. Love takes over and you're happy.

If you don't have abundance in every area of your life, you see what needs to be done. Bail out the negativity, the non-loving feelings.

Be loving. It's worth your life. Make loving an all the time, every time way of living. Watch the positive changes in your life.

I had a very profound experience one evening. A feeling of complete and total love, more than I had ever experienced before in my life, took me over completely. Like a river flowing from me, it seemed to have no direction or have no object but flowed out in all directions. It seemed to me to be more massive, stronger and larger than any flow, wider than any river I could imagine. It was like an exploding star that kept on exploding. That night only needed 2 hours sleep. I went to bed at 1:00AM woke at 3:00AM fully energized. The love kept flowing and flowing. It continued for most of the day, and partly into the next. It was an amazing and powerful experience.

— MM, California

Act From a Loving Place.

I finally found out confidence comes from ending the habit of beating myself up and loving myself all the time. Believe me it's made a big difference. I can't imagine living the old way again.

— RC, Illinois

When you're in a loving place you take the right action in your life. Whatever you say or do is effective. It works.

When you're loving, your action is correct action because it's action made in the now, in the present. It's action based on intuition. In love energy, all your mental noise, your garbage is out of the way. All your negative feelings are out of the way. Your action comes from a place of clarity.

Acting from non-love energy is wrong and harmful. It's acting from negativity, from non-love feelings. When action is taken from non-love

135

feelings it's action taken from your past. Negative, non-love feelings are from your past. When you're living in the present moment there aren't any non-love feelings. Non-love feelings are all automatic, reactive behavior you learned in the past.

When you act from a non loving place, the result is negative, of course. Negativity cannot generate anything positive.

Think of a few examples. You get mad at someone. After awhile, your anger quiets and guilt overcomes you. Anger and guilt are two negative, non-loving emotions that do nothing positive for you.

Fear is another example. You get scared so you act or you don't act because you're coming from fear. You end up in regret. You think, "I shouldn't have done that." "I shouldn't have said that." "I should have done that." "I should have said that." Fear and regret, two more non-loving feelings that don't do anything good for you.

What's the answer? The answer is to act from positive energy, to act from love and everything works out perfectly. When you act from positive energy, when you act from love, you're acting in harmony with the universe. You're acting from the present moment. So, whatever happens will be just right and everyone involved will benefit.

In the same way, acting from a loving place benefits your body. If you're living in non-loving feelings, you're living in a condition of dis-ease. You're living in disharmony. You're living in sickness.

Living in the positive energy of love is living in harmony and no one and nothing can bother you. Living from positive, love energy, is living in harmony with the universe.

That is the answer. Act from a loving place and everything you do will work out perfectly.

Love is the answer.

I have found out who I really am. I have been able to look deep inside me, and see the real me. Being only 18 years old, I have been exposed to a wonderful thing.

— BW, Virginia

My son was going through a rough time. He had gone back to his destructive, old habits. I kept going back and forth between letting go of disapproving of him and wanting to kick him out. One day, I just decided to be the love that I am. I then let the love expand to everyone in the house, then the neighborhood, then the city, then the whole world. I then thought of my son and only had love for him and all the disapproval was gone. That night, I told my son that if he didn't get back on track, he had to leave. No one likes to hear that, but my son is extreme when it comes to not wanting to hear it. However, because I was coming from a loving place without disapproval, he was very accepting of what I said. He started to really apply himself at work and is doing much better having dropped the destructive habits.

— BA, Texas

Love Yourself and All Else Will Follow.

This story is about when I was supposed to be teaching about prayer in Sunday School. A boy said that he couldn't yo-yo and sure enough he couldn't. Then I told him to say to himself that he could yo-yo and funny enough, he could. I then said, that's what prayer is — saying something nice to yourself about yourself.

That's the bottom line of all of it as far as I'm concerned: Love Yourself and all else will follow. Say something nice about yourself to yourself, love yourself, and your life will be beautiful beyond words. I realized that I have no problems when I am loving myself. In fact, everything goes smoothly for me and all those around me when I remember to love myself. Works pretty well when I am just loving others, but it works topnotch when I am loving myself and everybody else, too.

137

Loving yourself is automatically loving others. The trick is to keep remembering all that until it is the permanent condition of living.

— Mary Lowe, California

CHAPTER SIXTEEN

GET IN TOUCH WITH YOUR LOVE

The following quotations by Lester Levenson illuminate your understanding of the real nature of love. Each of these aphorisms brings a key theme about love into your awareness. Each of these statements are thoughts for your mind to digest, but even more importantly, energy for your whole being to absorb. Lester recommends that you read them slowly. Allow enough time for reflection and integration. Allow yourself enough time to practice the powerful gifts contained in these pages. You will discover for yourself a direct link to the source of your own wisdom. As Lester said, "You will come to know that you know."

The following quotations are from the book The *Ultimate Truth* by Lester Levenson.

Love — What is it?

Love is a feeling of givingness with no thought of receiving any return for it.

Love is allowing the other person to have exactly what they want, even though you cannot give it to them.

Love is giving with no strings attached.

Love is the natural inherent state of human beings.

Only by loving does love come to us. The more we love, the more love comes to us.

Love and giving are two words that are synonymous.

Love is an attitude, a feeling, and requires no action.

Love is a freeing of the other one.

Love is acceptance.

> *The more we develop love, the more we come in touch with the harmony of the universe, the more delightful our life becomes, the more beautiful, the more everything. It starts a cycle going in which you spin upward.*

Love is taking people as they are.

Love is loving the other one because the other one is the way the other one is.

Love is only understood when you love.

Love is trust.

When you love fully, you understand the other one fully.

Love is a feelingness of peace.

Love is identification. It is being the other one by identifying with the other one.

Love is what all beings are seeking through their every act.

Love is the answer to all problems.

When there are problems, if you would love more, they would disappear. When the love is complete, the problem dissolves immediately.

Love and understanding are the same.

Love is communing; it is communication.

Lending support, wanting for the other one what the other one wants, that is love.

The greatest help or giving one may give to another is to help the other to get the understanding of Truth. In this way, one gives the other the formula for happiness.

Love is a power. It is the cohesive force of the universe.

Love is attracting, integrating, and constructive and so affects anything that it is applied to.

Parliaments cannot right the world, but enough individuals feeling love can.

Almost all people mistake ego approval for love. Because it is not love, it is not satisfying. Consequently, one continuously needs and demands it. And, this produces only frustration.

Love is not sex.

Love is not an emotion.

People need each other and think it is love. There's no hanging onto, fencing in of the other when one loves.

Human love does not want to share its love with others but rather, wants its own personal satisfaction. Real love wants to share its love and the more it is shared, the more joyous it is.

There is no "longing for" in love, because longing for another is separation; love being oneness, it does not allow separation.

True love cannot be gotten through marriage. It must be there before marriage.

Love cannot be applied to one and not another. It's impossible to love one and hate another. When we love one more than another, that one is doing something for us. That is human love. When one loves people because they are nice to them, that too is human love.

True love is unconditional. In true love, one loves even those who oppose him or her.

We should love everyone equally.

It's impossible to get love. Only by loving can one feel love.

The more one looks for love, the more one doesn't love.

One should strive to love, never to be loved. To be loved brings temporary happiness and ego inflation.

When one loves fully, one can have no concept of not being loved.

To love our enemy is the height of love.

When love is felt for the enemy, it makes the enemy impotent, powerless to hurt you. If the enemy persists in trying to hurt you, the enemy will only hurt themselves.

One does not increase their love. One merely gets rid of their hate.

In a state of high love, one has a feeling of harmlessness and grants the other one the other one's beingness.

When you love fully, you feel you have everything.

Loving fully, one only sees love.

When one really loves, one can never be hurt.

Love has no personal angles.

Anytime one feels good, one is loving. Anytime one feels bad, one is not loving.

Love and egotism are opposites.

Love is selflessness.

Love is purity.

Love eliminates fear.

Love eliminates anxiety.

Love eliminates insecurity.

Love eliminates loneliness.

Love eliminates unhappiness.

Love attracts love.

Love is the means and the end.

Love is its own reward.

Love seeks its own likeness.

Love flourishes in love.

Love is contagious.

Love cannot be intellectualized.

The sweetness of love cannot be described. It must be experienced.

Full love is constant and can never be not. When attained, one only feels it, sees only it, hears only it. and thinks only it.

Love is patient and kind. Love is not jealous or boastful. It is not arrogant or rude. Love does not insist on its own way. It is not irritable or resentful. It does not rejoice at wrong, but rejoices in the right. Love bears all things, believes all things, hopes all things, endures all things.

Following are quotations from
The Way to Complete Freedom
by Lester Levenson

The real love is the love we feel for others. It is determined by how much we give ourselves to others.

Full love is identifying with every other human being.

When we identify with everyone, we treat everyone as we would treat ourselves.

Love is the balm, the salve that soothes and heals everything and all.

When you love, you lift others to love.

The most you can give is your love. It is greater than giving materiality.

When you understand people, you see that they are doing right in their own eyes. When you understand, you allow, accept. If you understand, you love.

When we love, not only are we happy but also our whole life is in harmony.

Happiness is equal to one's capacity to love.

If we love completely, we are perfectly happy.

There is always either love or lack of it.

When one is not loving, one is doing the opposite.

The highest love is when you become the other one. Identity is love in its highest form.

If you love your enemy, you have no more enemies.

The power and the effect of love is self obvious. Just try it!

If you look at it from your very own center, the words love, acceptance, identification, communication, truth, God, Self are all the same.

The original human state was all love. Troubles are due to humans covering over their natural state of love.

Love and discover that selflessness turns out to be the greatest good for yourself.

Love is effortless and hate requires much effort.

Apply love and every problem resolves.

Human love needs the other one. Divine love is giving to the other one.

Love equals happiness. When we are not happy, we are not loving.

The concept of possessiveness is just the opposite of the meaning of love. Love frees, possessiveness enslaves.

Love is a feeling of oneness with, of identity with, the other one. When there's full love you feel yourself as the other person. Then treating the other person is just like treating your very own self. You delight in the other one's joy.

Love is a tremendous power.

One discovers that the power behind love, without question, is far more powerful than the hydrogen bomb.

One individual with nothing but love can stand up against the entire world because love is so powerful. This love is nothing but the self. This love is God.

Love will give, not only all the power in the universe, it will give all the joy and all the knowledge.

The best way to increase our capacity to love is through understanding ourselves.

I think everyone knows the wonderful experience of loving one person, so you can imagine what it's like when you love seven billion people. It would be seven billion times more enjoyable.

Love is a constant attitude that evolves in us when we develop it. We should try practicing the love first on our family. Grant everyone in the family their own Beingness. Then apply it to friends, then strangers, then everyone.

The more we practice love, the more we love. The more we love, the more we practice love. Love begets love.

The more we develop love, the more we come in touch with the harmony of the universe, the more delightful our life becomes, the more beautiful, the more everything. It starts a cycle going in which you spin upwards.

The only method of receiving love is to give love because what we give out must come back.

The easiest thing in the universe to do is to love everyone. That is, once we learn what love is, it's the easiest thing to do. It takes tremendous effort not to love everyone and you see the effort being expended in everyday life. But when we love we're at one with all. We're at peace and everything falls into line perfectly.

In the higher spiritual love there is no self-deprivation. We don't have to hurt ourselves when we love everyone and we don't.

With love, there's a feeling of mutuality. That which is mutual is correct. If you love, you hold to that law.

Love is smothered by wrong attitudes. Love is our basic nature and natural thing. That's why it's so easy. The opposite takes effort. We move away from our natural self, cover it, smother it with concepts the opposite of love and then, because we're not loving, unloving comes back at us.

We feel the greatest when we love.

The real love wins the universe, not just one person, but everyone in the universe.

Behind the concepts of non-love, there is always the infinite love that we are. You can't increase it. All you can do it peel away the concepts of non-love and hatred so that this tremendous loving Being that we are is not hidden any more.

Love is an absolutely necessary ingredient on the path. If we ever expect to get full realization, we must increase our love until it is complete.

When you really love you can never feel parting. There is no distance because they're right there in your heart.

Only through growth do we really understand what love is.

When you really love, you understand the other one fully.

Love is an attitude that is constant. Love doesn't vary. Love cannot be chopped up.

All love, including human love, has its source in divine love.

Every human being is an extremely loving individual.

When you love, you think only the best for those you love.

The more you love, the more you understand.

There's one word that will distinguish the right love from the wrong love and that is giving.

You could hug a tree the same way as a person when you are very high. Your love permeates everything.

Total self sacrifice is the most selfish thing we can do. When self sacrifice is total we think only of others and are automatically in the Self.

Love is the state of the Self. It is something you are.

Consideration is a necessary part of love.

Anything but full love is, to a degree, hate.

Can you see why you can't be against anything? The ant is God, the enemy is God. If you're limiting any part, you're holding God away. Love cannot be parceled. Love has to be for all.

The greatest of all progress is love.

Your capacity to love is determined by your understanding.

If you don't trust someone, you don't love them fully.

If we love this world, we accept the world the way it is. We don't try to change it. We let it be. We grant the world its beingness. Trying to change others is injecting our own ego.

The more we love the less we have to think.

Being love is higher than loving. The devotees of God have no choice but to love, they are love.

Love is your Self. That is the highest love.

Love is an attitude that is constant. Love doesn't vary. We love our family as much as we love strangers. To the degree we are capable of loving strangers, to that degree we're capable of loving our family.

Love is togetherness.

Love is the Self. The Self doesn't love. Love is the Self. (Only in duality can you love.)

It's not loving, it's being love that will get you to God.

Love. Each one glorifies one's self by service rendered to others and must therefore, necessarily receive from others. Thus God flows back and forth and we delight in his exoticism. There is nothing so delectable as the spirit of givingness. It is intoxicating beyond any other experience capable to human beings.

Discover this:

Service is the secret to bathing in the ever-new joy of God. Service opens the doors to the greatest fields of beauty and charm wherein is enjoyed the nectars of the infinite variety of tastes, all blended into one drink, that of superlative love.

Come into the garden of the most delicious and everlasting joy by an everlasting desire to love and serve. Let go of the emptiness of selfishness. Fill yourself to the full with selfless love.

— Lester Levenson

CHAPTER SEVENTEEN

NOW YOU KNOW

At the beginning of the book, I told you the story of Lester Levenson. Few people ever really hear the story, though I tell it quite frequently.

The story of Lester Levenson is very simple. Let go of your non-love feelings. Look for your non-love feelings. Watch for your non-love feelings. Watch for your non-love thoughts, words, actions. When you see something in someone else that you do not like, look inside and see that non-love feeling in yourself.

All that is in your way to having all you would like to have is your non-love feelings. Seek out your non-love feelings and let them go. Constantly seek out your non-love feelings and let them go. Don't let non-love feelings get further than your nose when you see them. See a non-love feeling and let it go.

Accomplish being loving. Expand your capacity to love. And, expand your capacity to be happy, and healthy and abundant in every area of your life. Do it by letting go of the blocks to your love called, non-love feelings.

As you drop the non-love feelings more and more, the natural all loving being that you really are shines through and the whole world falls into your lap.

That's what Lester Levenson showed us.

Love is the answer. Love solves all. Love is what you are searching for in everything you do. And, where is love? It is right where you are. It is right inside of you covered up by the non-love feelings. All the love in the universe is right inside of you.

Experience all the love that you are. It is a decision. Decide to be the love that you are. Decide to be the loving being that you are by letting go of the non-love feelings.

That's the message of Lester Levenson. That's the message of this book. Love yourself. Love everyone. Lester showed us. In being love, we are happy, healthy, wealthy, successful and full of all the abundance in the universe.

Be love. Have it all.

Be that now.

Why settle for anything less than all the goodness the universe has to offer?

Love yourself. You deserve to have it all. You can have it all. Love yourself. Love yourself and find out.

Thank you for joining me on this journey of love.

Love, *Larry Crane*

At first as you discharge the negative, non-love energies, you find yourself experiencing more of the positive, loving feelings. Your life will improve in every way.
— Michael Hutchinson, Author

A Few More Words from Lester Levenson

Lester Levenson

Lester In His Own Words

Thank you. Greetings and love to each and every one of you. I think the biggest surprise tonight was to me. I didn't know I was going to talk until about ten minutes before eight this evening, when I was told I was going to be the surprise. So I began thinking, you know, what am I going to talk about? Talk about you? Or talk about me? And I realized, what's the difference?

We are all in the very same boat, called life. We're all doing, in my eyes, the exact same thing that I did. We are all looking for the summum bonum, the highest good, the ultimate place, the greatest happiness. And we're about it all the time, struggling for it, struggling for it, looking for it, looking for it, wondering, "Where is it?"

Well, back in 1952 I claimed I found the place. It's right where I am. It's right where you are. And all this looking for it everywhere, everyday, year in and year out, is such a waste of time. Why? It's right where you are. We're all here in this classroom called Earth, trying to discover something, the ultimate. And we're all looking for it externally, where it isn't! If we will only turn our direction back upon ourselves, we will discover it's right here, where I am, where you are, right in your very own Beingness.

I say, "Are you?" You say, "Yes." I say, "That's it." Do nothing else but that and you'll be in the ultimate good and the ultimate state of happiness.

But why don't you do it? You're so habituated into looking for it over there, over here, in him, in her, in this job, and it never is there. So we're all going through this same trip of trying to discover, "What is this all about? Where is my happiness?" And when we stop chasing after it out there and we turn inward, we discover that all these hard, negative, terrible feelings are only a feeling, and that it is possible to get rid of these feelings, by releasing them. And all these feelings are subconscious programs, every bit of them put in as pro-survival. It's not only fear that they say is fight-or-flight that is survival, all our feelings have been programmed-in to automatically keep us surviving. They keep us all the time looking out there, trying to survive; keep our mind active (subconsciously) 24 hours a day, so never for even one moment do we stop thinking and discover what we are.

If you could just stop your thinking for one moment, you will go through the most tremendous experience there is, that you are the totality of this universe, in your Beingness. That when your mind goes quiet, you automatically see, "I am the most terrific being there is in this universe. I am whole, complete, perfect. I always was, I am now, and I always will be."

So what is it that keeps us from being in that most delectable state there is? Simply, the accumulated programs called "feelings." All these negative feelings have us constantly struggling to survive, have us constantly looking away from this tremendous thing that we are. And all we need to do is to quiet that mind, and we become self-obvious to ourselves of this tremendous, loving being that we are.

How do we do it? I say it's simple, the Release Technique. It happens to be the fastest, the most effective, way there is to achieve this high state of being: where we are in total control of our universe, where every moment is a wonderful, wonderful moment, where it is impossible to be unhappy. And I say that's our natural state, when these negative feelings are released.

Someday you're going to do it. You're in the same boat, you're struggling, you're doing everything to achieve that happiness. But someday you'll get it, because you will never stop until you get there. But, if you want to do it faster, try our way. I promise you, you'll be very pleasantly surprised. Everything you're looking for is right where you are. All you need to do is to take off the blinders. Your vision is very blurred. You're looking through all these subconscious programs. When you release them, your vision becomes clear, you discover: you are the greatest. You're whole, you're complete, you're eternal. All your fear of dying disappears. And life is so comfortable after that. And there's no struggle, no struggle whatsoever, when you get these negative feelings up and out.

So I urge you to take this method, it's a tool. In one week's time there'll be a big change in you for the better. And from there on, you will continue to get better and better and better, lighter and lighter, happier and happier.

And this thing called Love is your basic nature. All the Love there is in the universe is right in your basic nature. And you'll discover that happiness, your happiness, equates to your capacity to love. And conversely, all your misery equates to your need to be loved. Just love, love, love, and you'll be so happy, and healthy, and prosperous.

But again, you need to lift out these non-love feelings. So, again, I urge you to try our way. I promise you you'll be very satisfied. Try it, you'll like it.

Thank you so much for coming.

A final word from Lester Levenson…

So, we have had a chance to talk heart to heart. I hope this has helped you. And, I want you to know there is much more help available. I have talked to you in a manner that is designed to provoke thinking that leads you to a new realization. I have talked to you in a way that attempts to reach the part of you that inherently and intuitively understands more than your intellect.

All this leads you to wisdom. Wisdom that is higher than intellectual knowledge.

If you have found these words of value, I suggest you go on and explore the do-it-yourself method I have developed that will show you how to increase your understanding every day. It is called the Release Technique. It will give you keys to self growth and allow you to keep it going from here on.

The Release Technique is based on the premise that each one of us has no limits except those that we hold onto subconsciously, and when we let go of our subconscious limitations, we discover that our potential is unlimited. Unlimited in the direction of health, happiness, affluence and materiality.

The Release Technique will help you achieve the kind of life you want, and even more importantly, it will assist you in achieving self realization. The Release Technique is a post graduate course to this book. Practice it and achieve the ultimate state.

— Lester Levenson

About the Author...

Larry Crane has been showing people what he learned from Lester Levenson for over 30 years. Mr. Crane is passionately determined to spread the message and the insights of Lester Levenson throughout the entire world.

Mr. Crane has taught thousands of people worldwide to love themselves with the Release Technique, the Abundance Course and numerous other advanced courses, books, audio CDs, and live weekend and seven day retreats. The Release Technique is a method of letting go of negative emotions, stress, and subconscious blocks that hold people back from having total abundance and joy in their lives. Mr. Crane has taught business people, sales people homemakers, teachers, psychiatrists, medical doctors in many specialties, psychologists, sports and entertainment celebrities and others too numerous to mention.

Mr. Crane has been featured in hundreds of articles in newspapers, magazines — including Time and TV Guide — and on television throughout the world.

Larry Crane

*Just love yourself.
It's the smartest thing
you can do.*

Love, Larry Crane

Gains from Applying What I Have Learned in this Book

Love Yourself Shows You the Way.
Lester's Release Technique Helps You:

- Feel love any time.

- Rid yourself of attachments and aversions.

- Discover the truth of your being.

- Awaken to your true nature.

- Have inner transformation.

- Clear away years of accumulated confusion.

- Have abundance in every way.

- Manifest your dreams into reality.

- Rid yourself of worry.

- Access answers from your higher self.

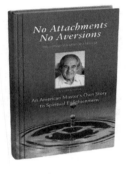

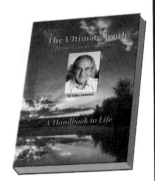

Total value of over $3,000 *for a limited time*

☐ **Yes!** Please rush me the **Abundance Course** Home Study audio set so I may examine it risk-free for 30 days.

☐ **Yes!** I read the LOVE YOURSELF book, so I qualify for the special price of $269. I save $226 off the regular price of $495.

☐ **Yes!** I also qualify for the **5 free audios**, a $125 value, mine to keep even if I return the material for a full refund.
(Less shipping and handling, of course.)

☐ Please rush me **CDs**.

☐ Enclosed is $281.95 ($269 plus $12.95 U.S. for shipping and handling)
(Overseas orders $316.95 U.S.—$269 plus $47.95 shipping and handling)
CA residents please add $24.88 (9.25%) sales tax. Total incl. ship/handling = $306.83
Sorry, we do not accept C.O.D. orders.

Make checks payable to Release Technique, LP

Total _____   ☐ Check ☐ Visa ☐ MasterCard

Your discount code is LOVE1.   ☐ Discover ☐ American Express

For fast action, call toll-free (24 hours a day): 1-888-333-7703
Outside the U.S. call: 1-541-957-4969

Name _____

Address _____City_____State_____Zip_____

Phone (day) _____ (eve.) _____
(In case we need to contact you if there is a question about your order.)

E-mail _____Occupation _____

Credit Card # _____ Expiration Date _____

Signature _____
Please be sure to check your address carefully and indicate any corrections.

Release Technique, LP
2800 Crusader Circle, Suite 10, Virginia Beach, VA 23453

DOUBLE GUARANTEE
If I am not convinced that the Abundance Course will work for me I may:
1) Receive Free coaching over the telephone, or 2) Return the course
within 30 days for a prompt refund and still keep the 5 free bonus audios.
(Less shipping and handling, of course.)

RECEIVE A FREE DOWNLOAD
WORTH OVER $25

The principles you've learned here of Loving Yourself and Letting the Other Person Have it Your Way have launched you on a journey leading to the fulfillment of all your dreams, go to www.loveyourselfbook.com claim your free download of an MP3 from Lester Levenson worth over $25 and reach the outer limits of your potential.